For Chuck, my closest friend and best critic, with love from Kate.
To Al, a special one who makes it fun to cook for two, with love from Barb.

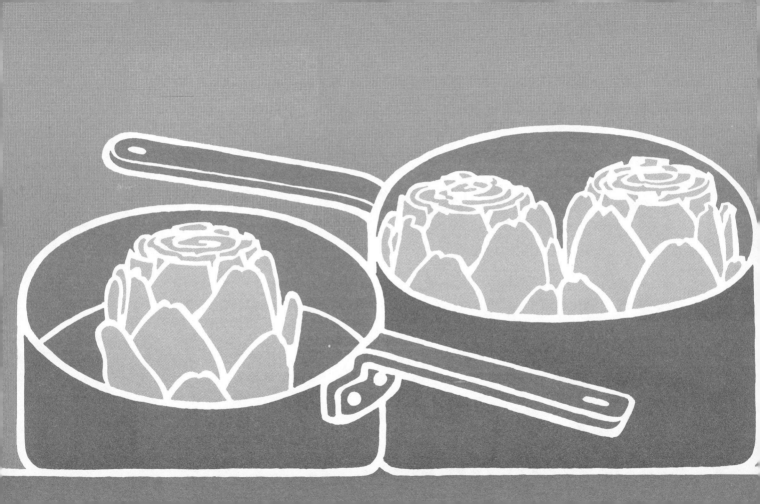

nitty gritty books

No Salt, No Sugar, No Fat
Fast and Delicious
Getting Started in the Kitchen
Brunch
My Cookbook
Family Favorites
Cookies
Cooking for 1 or 2
Chicken Cookery
Skillet Cookbook
Convection Oven
Household Hints
Seafood Cookbook
Quick Breads

Pasta & Rice
Yogurt
Cocktails & Hors d'Oeuvres
Casseroles & Salads
Food Processor Cookbook
Soups & Stews
Crepes & Omelets
Microwave Cooking
Vegetable Cookbook
Bread Baking
The Crockery Pot Cookbook
Classic Greek Cooking
Low Carbohydrate Cookbook
Kid's Cookbook

Cheese Guide & Cookbook
Miller's German
Quiche & Souffle
To My Daughter With Love
Natural Foods
Working Couples
Mexican
Fisherman's Wharf Cookbook
Barbecue Cookbook
Ice Cream Cookbook
Blender Cookbook
The Wok, a Chinese Cookbook
Fondue Cookbook

designed with giving in mind

Nitty Gritty Productions ● P.O. Box 5457 ● Concord, California 94524

Cooking for 1 or 2

by
Katherine Hayes Greenberg
Barbara Kanerva Kyte

Illustrated by Craig Torlucci

A Nitty Gritty Book*
Published by
Nitty Gritty Productions
P.O. Box 5457
Concord, California 94524

*Nitty Gritty Books-Trademark
Owned by Nitty Productions
Concord, California

Printed in the U.S.A.
By Mariposa Press
Concord, California
Edited by Maureen Reynolds

ISBN 0-911954-58-9
Library of Congress Catalog Card Number 80-81246

TABLE OF CONTENTS

INTRODUCTION

COOKING FOR ONE OR TWO can be as creative as cooking for a crowd. And there are advantages to cooking in small quantities. Marketing and preparing meals are much simpler, and with fewer people to consider it is easier to vary the menu, dinner hour and setting.

Our imaginative recipes are specially tailored to serve one or two. Many have variations and make-ahead suggestions. They are nutritious, economical and easy to prepare.

We hope our ideas and recipes will excite you and that you will look forward to eating alone or with a friend.

1

PLANNING AND MARKETING

Our planning and marketing tips will help you eliminate leftovers, as well as unnecessary trips to the grocery store.

Plan your weekly menu and make a shopping list taking into account basic nutrition, seasonal foods and weekly specials. For each day select foods from the four food groups: meats, fruits and vegetables, milk, and breads and cereals.

MILK

Select two or more servings of milk, buttermilk, cottage cheese, cheese, ice cream and yogurt.

FRUITS AND VEGETABLES

Select four or more servings of green and yellow vegetables and a variety of fruits.

MEATS

Select two or more servings of meat, poultry, eggs, fish, dried beans and nuts.

BREADS AND CEREALS

Select four or more servings of breads, cereals, rice, pasta and corn products.

2

TIPS:

- When you anticipate having a busy schedule, plan one of our meals that can be prepared quickly such as sandwiches or seafood or make a pot of soup ahead to heat and serve.
- When shopping, avoid the temptation to buy foods not on your list. Buy only what you plan to use and have room to store.
- Don't shop when you are hungry! You'll buy more than if you were not.
- Ask your grocer to divide large packages of meat or produce into smaller portions. Or divide large cuts of meat or poultry into smaller portions at home to freeze for several meals.
- Buy frozen vegetables and fruits loosely packed in plastic bags. Take out small portions as needed and keep the rest frozen.
- Purchase frozen chopped onions, green peppers, chives and lemon juice to have on hand.
- Plan to use perishable foods such as fish and berries within one or two days after shopping.

4

STORING FOODS

Proper food storage lengthens the time foods remain fresh. To prepare foods for the refrigerator, place them in covered containers or wrap them in foil or plastic to preserve freshness and flavor. Before freezing foods, place them in airtight containers leaving room for expansion or wrap them tightly with foil or freezer wrap. Do not refreeze meat, poultry or seafood. It destroys their flavor. Freeze foods in serving-sized portions or make your own frozen dinner by placing a meal on a divided foil tray. Cover the tray with foil and freeze. Most cooked foods may be frozen for up to two months.

BREAD — Freeze what you do not plan to use within a few days.

DAIRY PRODUCTS — Milk, eggs, sour cream and cottage cheese keep for five to seven days in the refrigerator. They should never be frozen. Store cheese and butter in the refrigerator for up to two weeks. Hard cheeses and butter may be frozen.

FRUITS — Ripen fruits at room temperature; then refrigerate them. Use ripe fruits within three days. Store apples and citrus fruits in the refrigerator for one week or more. Don't wash fruits until you are ready to use.

MEAT AND POULTRY — Refrigerate and use meat or poultry within two or three days after purchasing. May be frozen for up to six months.

SEAFOOD — Use fresh seafood within one or two days after purchasing. If wrapped well, it may be frozen for up to three months.

STAPLES — Refrigerate whole wheat flour, wheat germ, dried fruits and nuts. Store flour, sugar and honey, rice and pasta, cereals, herbs and spices at room temperature in sealed containers for up to one year in a cool, dark place. Other staples to have on hand are oil, vinegar, baking powder, baking soda, beef and chicken stock granules, salt, pepper and condiments.

VEGETABLES — Store vegetables in the refrigerator for five to seven days. Wash them just before you use them. To keep lettuce fresh, wash, wrap in paper towels and refrigerate. Store onions and potatoes in a cool, dark place, or in the refrigerator.

COOKWARE

It is not necessary to equip your kitchen with every appliance and cooking utensil. Purchase only what you need. Small appliances and "refrigerator to oven to table" cookware are convenient. For best results, use small bowls and pans when cooking small quantities. Organize your kitchen so that items that are used together are stored together. For easy cleanup use disposable foil pans or line baking and broiling pans with foil.

COOKING
6 and/or 8-inch frying pan
10-inch frying pan, with cover
1-quart saucepan, with cover
2-quart saucepan, with cover
3-quart saucepan, with cover
broiler pan with rack
1-quart casserole dish, with cover
vegetable steamer

MEASURING AND MIXING

set of mixing bowls (stainless steel or glass are best)
set of measuring cups (for both liquid and dry ingredients)
measuring spoons
rubber spatula
wooden spoons
wire whisk
rolling pin

BAKING

two custard cups
two 10-ounce souffle dishes
two 4-inch tart pans
two ramekins
8 x 8 x 2-inch baking pan

8-inch round baking pan
muffin pan
baking sheet
wire cooling rack
pot holders

FOOD PREPARATION
colander
strainer
spatula
slotted spoon
tongs
ladle
juicer
grater
peeler
slicing knife
paring knife
skewers
pepper grinder
plastic storage containers with covers
cutting board
can opener
kitchen timer

APPLIANCES
mixer
blender
toaster

OPTIONAL
garlic press
fondue pot and forks
wok
hibachi
electric frying pan
toaster oven
food processor
microwave oven

APPETIZERS

Appetizers can set the stage for dinner or they can become a light dinner. If the former is the case, provide an appetizer that contrasts delicately to the meal to be served. It should not be so spicy or rich as to overshadow the entree or leave you or your guests too full to enjoy the forthcoming meal. For example, a fresh slice of cantaloupe melon wrapped in prosciutto would appropriately begin a dinner consisting of Minestrone Soup, Veal Piccata and Baked Noodles Ricotta. If appetites are light, the weather is warm or you just don't feel like cooking, select an appetizer for two for dinner. Cubes of ham, cheese, cherry tomatoes and fruit threaded on a skewer make a complete light meal.

The Boursin, Cheese Ball and Pate refrigerate well for up to a week and a half. Make one of them on Monday and enjoy it several times that week with cocktails.

QUICK APPETIZERS

These appetizers are easy to make for one or two servings.
- Prepare an antipasto tray with an assortment of fresh or marinated vegetables, cheeses, cold sliced meats, olives and pickles.
- Wrap melon or papaya wedges with prosciutto.
- Wrap water chestnuts, chicken livers, shrimp or mushrooms with bacon and secure with a toothpick. Broil until bacon is crisp, turning once.
- Thread cubes of ham, cheese and cherry tomatoes or fresh fruit on a skewer.
- Top a 3-ounce package of cream cheese with chutney and serve with crackers.
- Serve shrimp and raw vegetables with Aioli mayonnaise, page 73.
- Marinate fresh mushrooms in Vinaigrette dressing, page 68. Serve with toothpicks.
- Cut corn or flour tortillas into wedges. Place in lightly buttered baking dish and bake at 400°F. until crisp. Sprinkle with grated Cheddar or Monterey Jack cheese. Return to oven. Bake until cheese melts.

HOT CRAB SPREAD

An elegant hors d'oeuvre for a special occasion. Serve with sesame or poppy seed crackers.

1 pkg. (3 ozs.) cream cheese
2 tbs. white wine
1/2 tsp. Dijon mustard
dash salt and pepper
1/2 cup cooked and flaked crab

Combine all ingredients, except crab, and warm slowly in saucepan. Stir in crab and heat through. Serve hot with crackers or bread rounds. Makes about 2/3 cup.

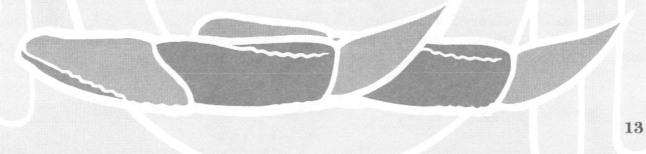

13

BOURSIN

A garlic and herb flavored cheese spread that keeps for several weeks in the refrigerator.

1 pkg. (3 ozs.) cream cheese, softened
2 tbs. sour cream
1/2 clove garlic, crushed
1 tbs. finely chopped green onions
1 tbs. finely chopped parsley
1/4 tsp. dried thyme, tarragon or dill
1/2 tsp. grated lemon peel (optional)
freshly ground pepper

Mix all ingredients together until smooth, using a mixer or food processor. Spread on crackers or stuff raw mushroom caps or cherry tomatoes with cheese mixture. Makes 1/2 cup.

CHEESE BALL

This hors d'oeuvre may be made several days before you serve it. It keeps well for up to two weeks in the refrigerator. Overlap slices of green and red apples around the Cheese Ball for an attractive cheese board.

1 pkg. (3 ozs.) cream cheese, softened
1/2 cup grated Cheddar cheese
1 tbs. dry sherry or brandy
dash Worcestershire sauce
dash garlic powder
chopped nuts

Combine all ingredients, except nuts, in a mixing bowl or the work bowl of a food processor. Beat or process until smooth. Form into ball. Roll cheese ball in chopped nuts. Wrap in plastic and refrigerate. Makes one small cheese ball.

GUACAMOLE

Not being able to obtain ripe fruits or vegetables from the market can be discouraging. Here's a tip to quicken the ripening of avocados: put them in a brown paper bag for a few days. They ripen much faster than just sitting on your windowsill.

1 ripe avocado, mashed
1 green onion, sliced
1 tbs. lemon juice
2 tbs. chopped and seeded tomato
dash Tabasco sauce
salt and pepper

Mix all ingredients together well. Chill until ready to serve. Serve with tortilla chips. Makes 3/4 cup.

Hints: Top tacos, burritos and enchiladas with guacamole. Do not puree in a blender or food processor. Mixture should be slightly lumpy.

PATE

Serve with crackers or French bread. Makes a good sandwich spread too.

1 tbs. butter
1/2 clove garlic, chopped
1 tbs. chopped onion
1/4 lb. chicken livers
2 tbs. dry sherry
salt and pepper

In small skillet, melt butter over medium heat. Add garlic, onion and chicken livers. Reduce heat to low and simmer for ten minutes. Pour contents of skillet into blender or food processor. Add sherry, salt and pepper. Blend or process until smooth. Pour into container and refrigerate for at least two hours. Keeps well for up to a week in the refrigerator. Makes 3/4 cup.

SOUPS AND SAUCES

With the addition of a roll and a tossed green salad, soup becomes a complete meal. Many of our soups can be served either hot or cold, providing you with more variety. Because soups are so easy to prepare, why not double or triple the recipe? The extra portions may be refrigerated for up to a week in a sealed container. Enjoy the soup several days later; its flavor has probably improved. But best of all, you don't have to cook. Soups and sauces also freeze well. Pour them into an airtight container and they will remain fresh for up to two months.

We've included a series of classic sauces, among them Hollandaise and Sweet and Sour, that will enhance vegetable and meat dishes and expand your recipe repertoire.

CREAM OF VEGETABLE SOUP CHART

Choose one of these light and luscious soups to start a meal or accompany a sandwich. They are equally delicious served cold.

1/2 cup chicken broth
1 tbs. chopped onion

1/3 cup light cream or milk
salt and pepper

BROCCOLI:
2 cups chopped
   broccoli
dash cayenne

CARROT:
1 cup peeled and sliced
   carrots
dash nutmeg

POTATO:
1 cup peeled and cubed
   potatoes
1 tsp. chopped parsley

Combine chicken broth, onion, vegetable and seasonings in saucepan. Bring to boil. Reduce heat. Cover and simmer 10 to 15 minutes, or until vegetable is tender. Pour into blender or food processor. Add cream, and blend until smooth. Serve hot or cold. Makes 1-1/4 cups.

ZUCCHINI SOUP

A great way to use a bountiful zucchini harvest.

1 slice bacon, cooked and crumbled, OR 1 tbs. bacon bits
4 cups sliced zucchini
1/4 cup chopped onion
1 clove garlic, chopped
1/2 cup beef broth
1/4 tsp. basil
salt and pepper
Parmesan cheese, grated

Combine all ingredients, except Parmesan, in saucepan. Simmer about 20 minutes, or until zucchini is tender. Puree in blender or food processor. Serve hot. Sprinkle with parmesan cheese. Makes 3 cups.

LENTIL AND SAUSAGE SOUP

A hearty soup that is even better the second day. Serve it with French bread and finish the meal with a crisp green salad.

1/2 cup dried lentils
3 cups beef broth
1/2 sliced leeks or onions
1/2 cup sliced carrots
1/4 cup sliced celery
1/2 cup grated potato
1 cup sliced garlic sausage

1 bay leaf
1 tsp. wine vinegar
dash thyme
salt and pepper
3 tbs. finely chopped parsley
  (optional)

Combine lentils and beef broth in saucepan. Bring to boil. Remove from heat. Cover and let stand one hour. Add remaining ingredients and simmer covered for one hour, or until lentils are tender. Remove bay leaf and serve hot. If desired, garnish with parsley. Makes one quart.

FRENCH ONION SOUP

For a light supper accompany this soup with a tossed green salad. Our Salad Chart, on page 52, will give you some ideas.

1 tbs. butter
1 medium onion, sliced
2-1/2 cups beef broth
salt and pepper
2 slices toasted French bread
1/4 cup grated Gruyere or Swiss cheese

Melt butter in small saucepan over medium heat. Add sliced onion. Saute until tender and golden brown. Add broth and simmer 15 minutes. Season with salt and pepper. Place toast in two heat-proof soup bowls. Pour soup over toast. Sprinkle with cheese. Place under broiler for a few minutes until cheese melts. Makes 2 servings.

MINESTRONE

A nutritious vegetable soup. Top with a spoonful of our Pesto, on page 91, and serve with French bread.

2 cups chicken broth
1 small zucchini, sliced
1 cup frozen mixed vegetables
1 tomato, peeled and chopped
2 tbs. chopped onion
1 clove garlic chopped

1/3 cup uncooked macaroni
1 can (8-3/4 ozs.) kidney beans, drained
1/4 tsp. oregano
1/4 tsp. basil
Parmesan cheese, grated

Bring broth to boil in saucepan. Add remaining ingredients, except Parmesan cheese. Reduce heat and simmer 15 mintues. Pour into serving bowls. Sprinkle with Parmesan cheese and serve. Makes 1 quart.

MANHATTAN CLAM CHOWDER

Keep these ingredients on hand for a quick meal.

1 slice bacon, cooked and crumbled, OR 1 tbs. bacon bits
2 tbs. chopped onion
1/4 cup sliced celery, optional
1 can (6-1/2 ozs.) minced clams, undrained
1 can (16 ozs.) peeled tomatoes, chopped and undrained
1 small potato, cubed
1 small carrot, chopped
dash thyme
salt and pepper
oyster crackers (optional)

Combine all ingredients, except crackers, in saucepan. Simmer covered for 30 minutes, or until vegetables are tender. If desired, serve with oyster crackers. Makes 1 quart.

25

GAZPACHO

A cold Spanish soup to serve on a hot summer day.

1 tomato, peeled and cut
into quarters.
1 can (12 ozs.) tomato juice
2 tbs. chopped green pepper
2 tbs. chopped onion
1/2 cup chopped cucumber
1 clove garlic, minced

1 tbs. oil
1 tbs. wine vinegar
salt and pepper
1 hard-cooked egg, finely chopped
   (optional)

Combine all ingredients, except hard-cooked egg in blender or food processor. Blend or process just until vegetables are pureed.

Chill several hours or overnight. Serve garnished with chopped egg, if desired. Makes 2-1/2 cups.

HOLLANDAISE SAUCE

An easy version of a classic sauce to serve with asparagus, broccoli or new potatoes.

2 egg yolks
1 tbs. hot water
1 tbs. lemon juice
dash nutmeg or cayenne
dash salt
1/2 cup hot melted butter

Run hot water over blender container to warm. Blend egg yolks, water, lemon juice and seasonings. Slowly pour in melted butter blending until thickened. Serve at once. Refrigerate extra sauce and bring to room temperature before serving. Makes 3/4 cup.

BEARNAISE SAUCE

A classic accompaniment to steak, Chateau Briand or salmon.

2 tsp. tarragon vinegar
1 tsp. chopped shallots or green onions
dash tarragon
1/3 cup Hollandaise sauce

Bring vinegar, shallots and tarragon to boil in small saucepan. Stir into Hollandaise sauce to blend. Makes about 1/3 cup.

29

SWEET AND SOUR SAUCE

This sauce is great on fresh, steamed broccoli, snow peas or carrots. To make it into a complete meal add chopped cooked pork or meatballs and serve over rice.

2 tsp. cornstarch
1 tbs. firmly packed brown sugar
1 can (8 ozs.) pineapple chunks
1/4 cup water
1 tbs. vinegar
1 tsp. soy sauce
1 tbs. chopped green pepper
1-1/2 cups chopped cooked pork or meatballs (optional)

Combine cornstarch, sugar and juice from pineapple chunks in saucepan. Add water, vinegar and soy sauce, stirring until smooth. Cook, stirring constantly over medium heat, until thick. Add remaining ingredients and meat, if desired. Continue cooking over low heat until meat is thoroughly heated. Makes 1-1/4 cups sauce.

BARBEQUE SAUCE

A savory sauce for basting spareribs or chicken either in the oven or on the barbeque. This sauce keeps well in the refrigerator for up to three weeks.

1 cup Tomato Sauce, page 32
1 tbs. lemon juice OR vinegar
1 tbs. molasses or firmly packed brown sugar
1 tbs. minced onion
1/2 tsp. Worcestershire sauce
1/4 tsp. chili powder
salt and pepper

Combine all ingredients in saucepan. Simmer 5 minutes. Makes one cup.

TOMATO SAUCE

Homemade tomato sauce is so much tastier than canned and takes only fifteen minutes to prepare. Fresh basil will add even more flavor to the sauce.

1 tbs. olive oil
2 tbs. chopped onion
1 cup peeled, seeded and chopped tomatoes (about 3 medium)
salt and pepper

Heat olive oil to medium-hot in saucepan. Add onion. Saute until tender. Add tomatoes, salt and pepper. Simmer 10 minutes. If desired, puree in blender or food processor. Makes 1 cup.

VARIATIONS

- 1/4 tsp. basil or oregano ⎫
- 1/2 clove garlic, crushed ⎬ Added before simmering for 10 minutes
- 2 tbs. chopped green pepper, sauteed with onion

SALSA

A zesty sauce for tacos, steaks, chicken or poached or scrambled eggs.

1 medium tomato, peeled, seeded and chopped
1 tbs. sliced green onion
1/8 tsp. oregano
1 tsp. vinegar
2 tsp. oil
1 tbs. chopped green chilies or ripe olives
dash Tabasco (optional)
dash salt

Mix all ingredients. Store up to one week in refrigerator. Makes 1/2 cup.

Hint: For Huevos Rancheros, place a warmed corn tortilla on a plate. Top with scrambled or poached eggs and Salsa. Garnish with sour cream, if desired.

SANDWICHES

Sandwiches can be exciting, tantalizing and even exotic. Let us introduce you to a few that will make old standbys such as bologna and peanut butter and jelly pale in comparison. How about a Hot Seafood English Muffin? It consists of a mound of Swiss cheese, sliced mushrooms, cooked baby shrimp and chopped green onions bound together with mayonnaise on an English muffin half. It's cooked until hot; then broiled until bubbly. Perhaps a Monte Cristo would pique your interest. Egg-dipped slices of bread enfold thinly sliced ham, turkey and Swiss cheese. This savory sandwich is then fried in butter until it attains a delicate, golden brown.

POCKET BREAD SANDWICH

for 1		for 2
1	pita or pocket bread round	2
1/2 cup	thinly sliced cooked roast beef, chicken or lamb	1 cup
1/2 cup	shredded lettuce or sprouts	1 cup
2 tbs.	chopped onion	1/4 cup
1 small	tomato, chopped	1 large
2 tbs.	plain yogurt or sour cream	1/4 cup
1/4 to 1/2 cup	avocado, chopped or Guacamole, page 16	1/2 to 1 cup

Cut pita round in half to make 2 pockets. If desired, wrap round(s) in foil and warm in 300°F. oven for 10 to 15 minutes. Stir together meat, lettuce, onion, tomato and yogurt. Spoon filling into pocket bread and top with avocado or Guacamole.

STUFFED TUNA ROLLS

A perfect picnic carry-along because they are great served cold.

for 1		for 2
1/2 can	1 can (6-1/2 ozs.) tuna	1 can
1/4 cup	grated Cheddar cheese	1/2 cup
1-1/2 tsp.	minced onion	1 tbs.
1 tbs.	chili sauce	2 tbs.
1 tbs.	relish	2 tbs.
1 tbs.	mayonnaise	2 tbs.
1-1/2 tsp.	lemon juice	1 tbs.
1 large	French roll(s)	2 large

Combine all ingredients, except roll(s), in mixing bowl. Stir until blended. Slice about 1 inch off the end(s) of French roll(s). Scoop out center of roll(s) and discard. Spoon tuna mixture into roll(s). Wrap roll(s) in foil. Bake for 30 minutes in 350°F. oven. Serve hot or cold.

TACOS

Complete this meal with refried beans and fresh fruit.

for 1		for 2
1	tortilla(s)	2
1-1/2 tsp.	oil	1 tbs.
1/4 lb.	ground beef or cooked shredded chicken	1/2 lb.
1-1/2 tsp.	chopped onion	1 tbs.
dash	chili powder	dash
1/4 cup	shredded lettuce	1/2 cup
2 tbs.	grated Monterey Jack or Cheddar cheese	1/4 cup
1/4 cup	chopped tomato	1/2 cup
1/4 to 1/2 cup	chopped avocado or Guacamole, page 16	1/2 to 1 cup
1 tbs.	sour cream	2 tbs.
	Salsa, page 33	

Place oil in skillet over high heat. When oil is hot, add tortilla(s), one at a time. Fry 30 seconds on each side. Drain well on paper towels. Fold in half. Place in warm oven until needed. In remaining oil, brown beef or chicken with onion and chili powder. Drain excess oil. Stuff tortilla(s) with beef or chicken and top with remaining ingredients.

Hint: Just about any kind of leftover meat, including beef, lamb or pork, can be used to stuff tacos.

39

BAGEL WITH TOPPINGS

for 1		for 2
1	bagel(s), split and toasted	2
1 ounce	cream cheese, softened	2 ounces
	one or more variations	
	(see below)	

Spread bagel with cream cheese and top with any of the following variations or a combination.

VARIATIONS

- smoked salmon
- capers
- chopped hard-cooked egg
- sliced olives
- sliced cucumber
- watercress or sprouts

- shredded carrot
- chopped nuts
- raisins
- chopped dates
- jam or honey

- sliced avocados
- sliced tomatoes
- poppy seeds
- sesame seeds
- baby shrimp

SLOPPY JOES

A hot and hearty sandwich to serve at a moment's notice. It goes nicely with the Coleslaw, on page 58.

for 1		for 2
1/4 lb.	ground beef	1/2 lb.
1-1/2 tsp.	chopped onion	1 tbs.
1-1/2 tsp.	chopped green pepper	1 tbs.
1/4 cup	Barbeque Sauce, page 31	1/2 cup
1 slice	Cheddar or American cheese	2 slices
1	bun(s), split and warmed	2

In a small skillet, brown beef over medium-high heat. Drain fat. Add onion, pepper and Barbeque Sauce. Cover and simmer 15 minutes. Spoon meat over half of bun, top with cheese and broil until cheese melts. Top with other half of bun.

HOT SEAFOOD ENGLISH MUFFIN

Any cooked fish may be stirred into this savory spread.

for **1**   for **2**

for 1		for 2
1/4 cup	grated Swiss cheese	1/2 cup
1/4 cup	sliced mushrooms	1/2 cup
1 tsp.	chopped green onions or parsley	1 tbs.
1/4 cup	cooked shrimp, crab or tuna	1/2 cup
2 tbs.	mayonnaise	1/4 cup
1	English muffin(s), split	2

Combine all ingredients in a mixing bowl. Stir until blended. Spread over English muffin(s). Bake 10 minutes in 400°F. oven. Then broil until bubbly.

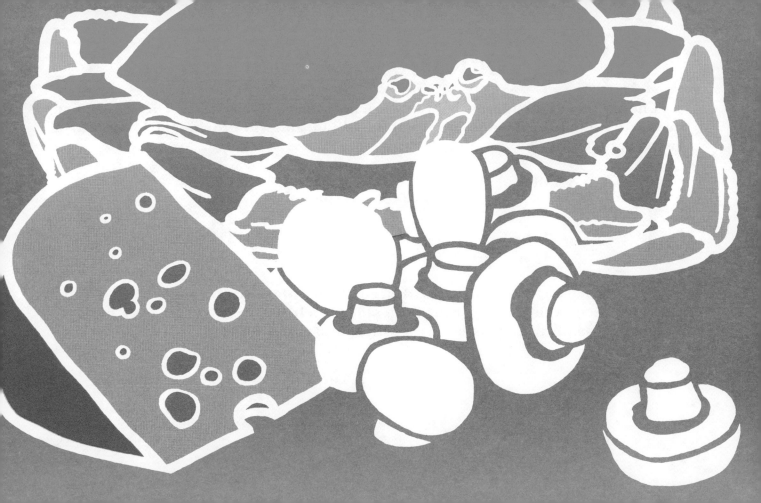

GRILLED SANDWICH

Choose any of the fillings below as a center for your sandwich. The egg-dipped bread will serve to seal in the flavors of the filling, and will provide the bread with a crusty, golden exterior.

for 1

		for 2
2 slices	bread	4 slices
	Filling (see next page)	
1	egg(s)	2
1 tbs.	milk	2 tbs.
1 tsp.	butter	2 tsp.

Place filling on bread and top with second slice of bread. Beat egg(s) with milk. Turn sandwich in mixture to coat both sides. Melt butter in skillet over medium heat. Brown sandwich, pressing down with spatula after turning.

FILLINGS

MONTE CRISTO — 1 slice of Swiss cheese and one or more slices of ham, chicken or turkey. Also, try one slice each of chicken or turkey AND ham.

RUEBEN — 1 slice of Swiss cheese, several slices of corned beef, 2 tablespoons or more of sauerkraut and 1 tablespoon or more of Thousand Island Dressing, page 72, on 2 slices of rye bread. Place on bread in order listed. Top with remaining slice of rye.

ITALIAN — 1 or more slices of Mozzarella cheese and as many slices of salami as desired.

HERB GARDEN — 1 slice Cheddar cheese, 2 or 3 slices of tomato. Sprinkle with dill, dip in egg batter and grill.

CLUB SANDWICH

Serve this with Bean Salad on page 54.

Serve this with Bean Salad on page 54.

for 1			**for 2**
3 slices	bread	6 slices	
2 to 3 tbs.	butter or mayonnaise	4 to 6 tbs.	
2	lettuce leaves	4	
4 to 6	tomato slices	8 to 12	
2	pineapple slices (optional)	4	
2 to 4 slices	chicken, turkey or ham	4 to 8 slices	

Toast bread, if desired. Spread one side of each slice with butter. Arrange lettuce leaves, tomato slices, pineapple slices and chicken slices on buttered side of two slices of bread. Stack bread, one on top of the other, ending with plain slice. Cut in half diagonally twice, creating an "X" on the bread.

PIZZA

Some people are purists, and prefer theirs with only a light sprinkling of cheese. Others feel cheated if theirs doesn't contain vast quantities of everything traditionally used for topping pizza—including anchovies. However you like your pizza, you'll enjoy this recipe.

1/2 package active dry yeast
1/2 cup warm water (about 110°F.)
1-1/4 cups flour
1/2 tsp. sugar
1/4 tsp. salt
1 tbs. oil
Pizza sauce, see next page
8 ounces Mozzarella cheese, grated
Variations, see next page

In mixing bowl, combine yeast with warm water. Stir until dissolved. Add flour, sugar, salt and oil. Mix well. Knead dough until smooth and elastic, adding more flour if dough is sticky. This will take about 10 minutes. Place in greased bowl turning to coat top. Cover with plastic wrap and a towel. Place in draft-free area. Let rise 1 hour. Punch down dough. Roll out to form 12-inch circle. Place on greased baking sheet and pinch edges to form a slight rim. Bake in 425°F. oven for 5 minutes. Spread pizza sauce over crust, top with variations and cheese. A food processor is convenient for grating cheese and slicing the variations. Bake 15 minutes, or until cheese is bubbly and crust is golden. Makes one small pizza.

PIZZA SAUCE

1/2 cup Tomato Sauce, page 32
1/2 clove garlic, crushed
1/4 tsp. oregano
1/4 tsp. basil

Combine all ingredients in saucepan and simmer for 5 minutes.

VARIATIONS

- sliced fresh mushrooms
- sausage or ground beef, cooked and crumbled
- pepperoni, sliced
- green pepper, sliced
- sliced olives
- anchovies

49

SALADS

Salads have become increasingly popular over the last few years. It seems everyone is more diet conscious, whether to lose weight or simply to eat more nutritiously. Salads make it possible for people to remain on their regimes without monotony or boredom. They make an appearance, in one form or another, at almost every lunch and dinner. If fact, some would consider a meal incomplete without a salad.

However you view salads, they are a boon to busy people. Simply by keeping a few things on hand, such as canned tuna, salmon, crab or shrimp and fresh greens, you have the makings of a salad. Be creative and learn to use your leftovers too. If you have boiled potatoes and string beans the night before and couldn't finish them, marinate the leftovers in vinaigrette overnight. The next evening, place them on a bed of lettuce. Add any of the following to the salad and you have created a salad Nicoise: 1 chopped hard-cooked egg, 1 tablespoon chopped olives, 1 tablespoon capers, 1 tablespoon chopped green onion, tomato slices and sliced mushroom.

SALAD CHART

Select one or more for your own salad. Toss with one of our dressings.

GREENS	VEGETABLES	PROTEIN	GARNISHES
iceberg lettuce	carrots (cooked or raw)	beef	green onion
romaine lettuce	tomatoes	chicken	red onion
red leaf lettuce	celery	ham	bacon, cooked and crumbled
butter lettuce	green pepper	salami	croutons
spinach	avocado	seafood	olives
cabbage	cauliflower (cooked or raw)	cheese	capers
endive	radishes	hard-cooked eggs	herbs
watercress	cucumber	nuts and seeds	beets

GREENS	VEGETABLES	PROTEIN	GARNISHES
	mushrooms (cooked or raw)	garbanzo beans	alfalfa or bean sprouts
	zucchini (cooked or raw)	kidney beans	red cabbage
	broccoli (cooked or raw)		water chestnuts
	asparagus (cooked or raw)		cooked bulgar
	green beans (cooked or raw)		
	artichoke hearts (cooked and marinated, if desired)		
	corn (cooked or raw)		
	peas (cooked or raw)		
	snow peas		

53

BEAN SALAD

Bean salad keeps for several weeks in the refrigerator. We add it to tossed green salads and sandwiches. Blue cheese or Roquefort Dressing, page 67, contrast exceptionally well with Bean Salad served with lettuce.

1 can (8 ozs.) kidney beans
1 can (8 ozs.) garbanzo beans
1 jar (6 ozs.) marinated artichoke hearts, undrained
small onion, sliced
3 tbs. wine vinegar
1 tbs. sugar
1/4 tsp. salt
1/2 tsp. celery seed
1/2 tsp. mustard seed

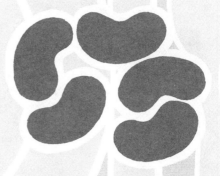

Rinse beans with water and drain. In a mixing bowl, combine all ingredients. Chill several hours or overnight before serving. Makes 3 cups.

TOSTADA SALAD

for 1

for 2

for 1		for 2
1 cup	shredded lettuce	2 cups
1 cup	refried beans	2 cups
dash	chili powder	1/4 tsp.
dash	cumin	1/4 tsp.
dash	garlic powder	1/4 tsp.
1	ripe avocado, mashed	2
1 tbs.	sour cream	2 tbs.
2 tbs.	sliced ripe olives	1/4 cup
2	green onions, sliced	4
1/2 cup	Cheddar cheese, shredded	1 cup
1 small	tomato, chopped	1 medium
	tortilla chips	

Arrange lettuce on plate. Mix beans with seasonings and spread over lettuce. Combine avocado with sour cream and spread over beans. Layer remaining ingredients over avocado. Serve with tortilla chips.

55

SPINACH SALAD

Serve this salad as an accompaniment to an entree or as the main dish. Choose either the Sweet and Sour or Soy Sesame Dressing to top it.

for 1			for 2
1/2 bunch	fresh spinach		1 small bunch
1/4 cup	bean sprouts		1/2 cup
1/4 cup	sliced mushrooms		1/2 cup
1/2	chopped hard-cooked egg		1
1 slice or 1 tbs.	bacon, cooked and crumbled		2 slices or 2 tbs.
1/2	green onion, sliced		1

Wash and dry spinach. Tear into bite-sized pieces in salad bowl. Add remaining ingredients. Combine ingredients for dressing. Mix well. Toss salad with dressing. Dressing may be prepared ahead. Serve salad as soon as it has been dressed.

SWEET AND SOUR DRESSING

2 tbs. oil
1/2 tsp. sugar
1 tbs. catsup
1 tbs. wine vinegar
1/2 tsp. Worcestershire sauce
salt and pepper

SOY SESAME DRESSING

2 tbs. oil
1 tbs. lemon juice
1 tsp. soy sauce
1 tbs. toasted sesame seed
1 tsp. honey
1/2 clove garlic, crushed
dash cayenne (optional)
salt and pepper

57

COLESLAW

A food processor will make quick work of the cabbage and carrots. Great with barbequed meats or poultry.

for 1

for 1		for 2
2/3 cup	shredded cabbage	1-1/3 cups
2 tbs.	shredded carrot or chopped apple	1/4 cup
1 tbs.	raisins (optional)	2 tbs.
1/4 tsp.	Dijon mustard	1/2 tsp.
1/2 tsp.	vinegar or lemon juice	1 tsp.
2 tbs.	mayonnaise or sour cream	1/4 cup
1/8 tsp.	celery seed	1/4 tsp.
	salt and pepper	

Combine all ingredients in a mixing bowl. Toss together to mix thoroughly.

POTATO SALAD

New potatoes are best for salads because they will not break apart when you toss them. Potato Salad can easily be made into a complete meal by adding 1/2 cup or more of diced, cooked ham or sausage.

2 cups cooked potatoes (3 medium), sliced or cubed
1 tsp. minced onion
1/3 cup mayonnaise
1 hard-cooked egg, chopped
1 tsp. vinegar
salt and coarsely ground pepper
2 tbs. sliced celery
2 tbs. chopped sweet pickles } OR { 1/2 clove garlic, crushed
1/2 tsp. celery seeds   2 tbs. chopped green pepper
                                      1 tbs. chopped parsley

Combine all ingredients in a mixing bowl. Toss gently until blended. Serve warm or chilled. Makes 2 servings.

Hint: Don't let it remain at room temperature for more than 45 minutes.

59

ROQUEFORT AND FRUIT SALAD

The strong flavor of the Roquefort cheese contrasts nicely with the apples and grapes. Serve this salad on a lettuce leaf.

for **1**

	for 1		for 2
1	apple, coarsely chopped	2	
1/2 cup	grapes	1 cup	
2 tbs.	broken walnuts	1/4 cup	
1 tbs.	Roquefort or blue cheese, crumbled	2 tbs.	
2 tbs.	sour cream	1/4 cup	

for **2**

In a mixing bowl, toss apples, grapes and walnuts together. Add remaining ingredients. Mix gently until combined.

CRAB LOUIS

for 1		for 2
	lettuce leaves	
1 cup	shredded lettuce	2 cups
1/2 cup	cooked crab meat or shrimp	1 cup
1	hard-cooked egg(s), quartered	2
1	small tomato, quartered	2
4	cooked asparagus spears (optional)	8
1 small	avocado, sliced (optional)	1 large
	lemon wedges	
	Thousand Island Dressing, page 72	

Arrange lettuce leaves on plate(s). Top with shredded lettuce and crab. Garnish with remaining ingredients. Spoon Thousand Island dressing over all.

CHICKEN AND FRUIT SALAD

Ham may be used instead of chicken in this refreshing salad.

for 1		for 2
1/2	pineapple or melon	1 whole
1/2 cup	seedless grapes	1 cup
1/2	banana, sliced	1 whole
2 tbs.	flaked coconut	1/4 cup
2 tbs.	sliced almonds	1/4 cup
3 tbs.	chopped dates (optional)	1/3 cup
1/2 cup	cubed cooked chicken or ham	1 cup
2 tbs.	lemon or orange yogurt	1/4 cup
dash	ginger	1/4 tsp.

Cut pineapple in half. Remove fruit leaving 1/2-inch shell. Cut fruit in chunks. If using melon, cut in half zig-zag fashion. Remove and discard seed. Scoop out fruit using a melon baller. Combine either pineapple chunks or melon balls with remaining filling ingredients. Stir well. Spoon filling into fruit shells.

STUFFED TOMATOES

| 1 | large tomato(es) | 2 |

Slice tops off tomato(es). Set aside. Scoop out seeds carefully without breaking through skin(s). Sprinkle with salt. Turn upside down and let drain 20 minutes. Stuff with Curried Egg Salad or Rice Salad.

CURRIED EGG SALAD

1-1/2 tbs.	mayonnaise	3 tbs.
1	hard cooked eggs, chopped	3
1/2	sliced green onion	1
dash	curry powder	dash
1/4 tsp.	soy sauce	1/2 tsp.
1/2 tsp.	lemon juice	1 tsp.
1-1/2 tsp.	chopped parsley	1 tbs.

Combine all ingredients, except parsley, in a mixing bowl. Toss gently to blend. Garnish with parsley, if desired.

RICE SALAD

for
1

		for 2
1/3 cup	cooked rice	2/3 cup
1 tbs.	mayonnaise or sour cream	2 tbs.
1 tsp.	capers	2 tsp.
1/4 cup	cooked shrimp (optional)	1/2 cup
	salt and pepper	
1-1/2 tsp.	chopped parsley (optional)	1 tbs.

Combine all ingredients, except parsley, in a mixing bowl. Toss gently to blend. Garnish with parsley, if desired.

65

CAESAR SALAD

for 1		for 2
1 clove	garlic	1 clove
1/2 small head	romaine lettuce	1 small head
1 tbs.	oil	2 tbs.
	salt and pepper	
1	egg yolk	1
1-1/2 tsp.	lemon juice	1 tbs.
1 tbs.	croutons	2 tbs.
1 tbs.	grated Parmesan cheese	2 tbs.
1/2	anchovy (optional)	1

Rub salad bowl with cut garlic clove. Tear lettuce into bite-sized pieces in salad bowl. Add oil, salt and pepper. Toss to coat lettuce leaves. Add egg yolk and lemon juice and toss throughly. Toss again with croutons and cheese.

BLUE CHEESE DRESSING

A flavorful dressing to spoon over crisp salad greens.

2 tbs. crumbled blue cheese or Roquefort
1/3 cup mayonnaise or sour cream
2 tbs. milk
dash garlic powder (optional)
salt and pepper

Combine all ingredients in a mixing bowl. Stir to blend. Chill. Makes 1/2 cup.

67

VINAIGRETTE DRESSING

The proportion of vinegar to oil may be varied according the acidity of the vinegar and the food to be dressed. Vegetables, such as cherry tomatoes and broccoli, green beans, asparagus or Brussels sprouts cooked until just tender, are great dressed with this Vinaigrette.

6 tbs. olive oil
2 tbs. wine vinegar or lemon juice
salt and pepper

Combine oil, vinegar, salt and pepper with any of the following variations. Mix thoroughly. Makes 1/2 cup.

VARIATIONS

Add one or more of the following:

- 1/2 clove garlic, crushed
- 1 tsp. chopped chives or parsley
- 1/8 tsp. dry mustard OR 1/2 tsp. Dijon mustard
- 1/4 tsp. tarragon, dill or basil (fresh is best)
- 1 tbs. grated Parmesan cheese
- 1 tsp. capers

YOGURT DRESSING

Toss with thinly sliced cucumbers or zucchini.

1/3 cup plain yogurt
1 tsp. chopped chives or green onion
dash dill
salt and pepper

Combine all ingredients in a mixing bowl. Stir until blended. Chill. Makes 1/3 cup.

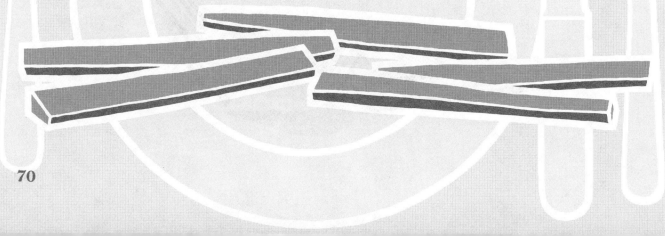

FRUIT DRESSINGS

Dress up a fresh fruit compote with one of these flavorful additions. A melon ball salad, consisting of cantalope, honeydew and watermelon would go well with either of these dressings.

POPPY SEED DRESSING

2 tbs. oil
1 tbs. lemon juice

1 tbs. honey
1/2 tsp. poppy seeds

1/8 tsp. dry mustard

Combine all ingredients in a mixing bowl. Stir to blend. Chill. Makes 1/4 cup.

SOUR CREAM DRESSING

1/4 cup sour cream
1 tbs. honey

1 tbs. orange juice
dash ginger

Combine all ingredients in a mixing bowl. Stir to blend. Chill. Makes 1/3 cup.

MAYONNAISE VARIATIONS

Mayonnaise is a versatile dressing. Many sauces, dips and salad dressings use it as their base. Here are a few of the more popular "variations on a theme."

THOUSAND ISLAND DRESSING

Serve this with Shrimp or Crab Louie.

1/4 cup mayonnaise
1 tbs. milk
1 tbs. chili sauce
freshly ground pepper

Combine all ingredients in a mixing bowl. Stir to blend. Chill. Makes 1/3 cup.

AIOLI OR GARLIC MAYONNAISE

Makes an excellent dip for artichokes, crab and shrimp. Let a dollop of it melt on top of fresh steamed vegetables, such as asparagas or new potatoes.

1/4 cup mayonnaise   1/4 tsp. Dijon mustard   1/2 clove garlic, crushed

Combine all ingredients in a mixing bowl. Stir to blend. Chill. Makes 1/4 cup.

TARTAR SAUCE

Any kind of fish or shellfish may be dipped into this classic sauce.

1/4 cup mayonnaise   2 tsp. finely chopped green onion or parsley
2 tbs. finely chopped pickle   1 tsp. lemon juice

Combine all ingredients in a mixing bowl. Stir to blend. Chill. Makes 1/3 cup.

EGGS AND CHEESE

Pound for pound, eggs are one of the least expensive forms of protein available. Additionally, almost every dish made with eggs is simple to prepare and cooks quickly, in comparison with meat, poultry and fish recipes. The spectrum of ways any egg dish can be varied is almost limitless. Bearing witness to this are the increasing number of omelet houses springing up around the country. These restaurants base their menus around this supremely versatile dish, knowing that they can please even the most jaded palate with their exotic creations.

A natural go-together with eggs, cheese is present in literally hundreds of forms. Since it has become so popular in the last few years, more unusual varieties are available at your local market. For an even bigger selection, visit a delicatessen or wine and cheese shop in your area.

OMELET

for 1			for 2
2 tsp.	butter	1-1/2 tbs.	
2	eggs	4	
1 tbs.	milk or water	2 tbs.	
dash	parsley, tarragon or dill	1/4 tsp.	
	salt and pepper		
	Filling (see below)		

Prepare filling ingredients. Set cheese aside. Combine all other filling ingredients in a small skillet or saucepan and keep warm while you prepare the omelet. In mixing bowl, beat eggs with milk, parsley, salt and pepper. Heat butter in an 8-inch omelet pan or skillet over high heat until butter sizzles. Be careful not to let butter burn. Pour egg mixture into pan. (If making 2 omelets, pour only half of egg mixture into pan. Prepare one, 2 egg omelete at a time.) Tilt pan to spread mixture up around edges. Loosen edges of omelet as it cooks to distribute uncooked portion underneath. When the top of the omelet is set into a soft custard, spoon filling over middle third of omelet. Lift each third of unfilled sides of omelet over filling. Slide out of pan onto a plate to serve.

FILLING

for

1

for 1		for 2
2 tbs.	grated cheese, such as Cheddar, Monterey Jack or Swiss	1/4 cup
2 tbs.	diced cooked vegetables, such as asparagas, zucchini, tomatoes, potatoes, broccoli or squash	1/4 cup
2 tsp.	bacon bits	1-1/2 tbs.
2 tsp.	chopped chives or green onions	1-1/2 tbs.
1/4 cup	sliced mushrooms, sauteed	1/2 cup

for

2

CHILI RELLENOS CASSEROLE

for 1		for 2
1/2 can	1 can (4 ozs.) whole green chilies	1 can
1/4 cup	grated Monterey Jack cheese	1/2 cup
1/4 cup	grated Cheddar cheese	1/2 cup
1	egg(s)	2
1/4 cup	sour cream	1/2 cup
1/3 cup	milk	2/3 cup
dash	salt	1/4 tsp.
1-1/2 tbs.	flour	3 tbs.
dash	baking powder	1/8 tsp.
	Salsa, page 33 (optional)	

Slit chilies lengthwise and remove seeds. Arrange in buttered baking dish. Sprinkle cheese over chilies. Mix remaining ingredients together and pour over chilies.* Bake in 350°F. oven for 40 minutes, or until set. Top with Salsa if desired.

*May be made ahead to this point. Chill up to one day before baking.

CHEESE STRATA

A light and delectable dish which may be varied by using different cheeses.

for 1

for 1		for 2
1 slice	French bread, crusts removed	2 slices
1 tsp.	butter	2 tsp.
1/3 cup	grated Cheddar cheese	2/3 cup
1	egg(s)	2
2 tbs.	dry white wine	1/4 cup
dash	Tabasco or nutmeg	dash
2 tbs.	Tomato Sauce, page 32 (optional)	1/4 cup

for 2

Spread butter over bread and place in buttered ramekin. Sprinkle cheese over bread. In mixing bowl, beat together egg(s), wine and Tabasco sauce. Pour mixture over cheese.* Bake in 350°F. oven for 30 minutes. Top with Tomato Sauce if desired.

*May be made ahead to this point. Chill up to one day before baking.

79

CHEESE SOUFFLE

An elegant way to use leftover meats and vegetables.

for 1		for 2
1-1/2 tsp.	butter	1 tbs.
1-1/2 tsp.	flour	1 tbs.
3 tbs.	milk or light cream	1/3 cup
1/3 cup	grated Cheddar cheese	2/3 cup
1	egg yolk(s)	2
dash	nutmeg, cayenne or dry mustard	dash
	salt and pepper	
1	egg white(s)	2
	Variation (see next page)	

Melt butter in saucepan over medium heat. Stir in flour. Let bubble 30 seconds. Add milk. Cook, stirring until thick. Add cheese. Stir until melted. Remove from heat. Mix in egg yolks, seasonings and variation.* Beat egg whites until they form moist peaks. Fold egg whites into yolk mixture. Spoon into 1 or 2 buttered 10-

ounce souffle dishes. Bake 20 minutes in 350°F. oven. Serve immediately.

VARIATIONS

Add one or more of these ingredients to your souffle before you bake it.

for
1

		for 2
1 tbs.	minced chives or green onions	2 tbs.
2 tbs.	chopped cooked vegetable	1/4 cup
2 tbs.	chopped cooked meat, poultry or seafood	1/4 cup
1 tbs.	cooked and crumbled bacon or bacon bits	2 tbs.

*May be made ahead to this point. Refrigerate for up to one day before baking. Bring to room temperature before folding in egg whites.

QUICHE

for
1

for
2

half recipe		whole recipe
	single crust pastry, page 174	
1	beaten egg(s)	2
1/4 cup	light cream, milk or plain yogurt	1/2 cup
1/4 cup	grated cheese such as Swiss or Cheddar	1/2 cup
1/4 cup	chopped meat, poultry, seafood or vegetable	1/2 cup
dash	dill, basil or tarragon salt	1/4 tsp.

Line one or two 4 1/2-inch tart pan(s) with pastry. Prick pastry shells all over with fork. Bake for 5 minutes in 425°F. oven. Beat remaining ingredients together in a mixing bowl.* Pour into prebaked pastry shell(s). Bake in 350°F. oven for 30 minutes, or until knife inserted into center comes out clean.

*May be made ahead to this point. Chill filling ingredients up to one day before baking.

82

QUICHE WITH NUTS

Nuts provide a nice contrast to the creamy texture of quiche. Substitute any one of these combinations for the 1/2 cup cooked chopped meat called for in the recipe on the preceding page.

- 2 tbs. sliced almonds with 1/2 cup cooked, chopped chicken
- 2 tbs. chopped cashews with 1/2 cup cooked, sliced zucchini
- 2 tbs. chopped walnuts with 1/2 cup cooked, sliced broccoli

QUICHE LORRAINE

- 1/2 cup grated Swiss cheese
- 2 slices bacon cooked and crumbled, or 2 tbs. bacon bits
- dash nutmeg

Substitute above ingredients for cheese, meat and herb in basic quiche recipe.

CHEESE ENCHILADA

Refried beans or Rice Verde, on page 97, make a nice accompaniment to this dish.

Refried beans or Rice Verde, on page 97

for 1		for 2
1 tbs.	oil	2 tbs.
2	tortillas	4
2 tbs.	chopped onion	1/4 cup
1/2	clove garlic, crushed	1
1/2 cup	Tomato Sauce, page 32	1 cup
dash	cumin	1/4 tsp.
dash	chili powder	1/4 tsp.
	salt and pepper	
1 cup	grated Cheddar cheese	2 cups
1	hard-cooked egg(s), chopped	2
1	green onion, sliced	2
1/4 cup	sliced ripe olives	1/2 cup

Heat oil in pan to medium-high. Fry tortillas lightly on both sides. Place on paper towels to drain. Reduce heat to medium-low. Saute onion and garlic in remaining oil until tender. Add Tomato Sauce and seasonings. Stir until mixture is heated through. Dip tortillas in sauce. Combine half of cheese, egg(s), onion and olives in a mixing bowl. Divide mixture among tortillas and fill. Roll tortillas to enclose filling and place in lightly greased baking dish. Top with remaining sauce and cheese.* Bake in 350°F. oven for 15 minutes, or until hot and bubbly.

*May be made ahead to this point. Chill for up to two days before baking.

CHEESE FONDUE

The word fondue is derived from the French word "fondre," which means to melt. The Swiss claim credit for the origin of fondue.

for 1

for 2

for 1		for 2
2 ozs.	Swiss cheese, grated	4 ozs.
2-1/2 ozs.	Gruyere, grated	5 ozs.
1 tbs.	flour	2 tbs.
1/2 cup	white wine	1 cup
1 tbs.	sherry	2 tbs.
dash	nutmeg	dash
	French bread cubes	
	ham cubes (optional)	
	apple cubes (optional)	

Shake cheese with flour in plastic bag. Let stand at room temperature for at least two hours. Heat wine in saucepan until bubbles start to rise. Add cheese and stir until blended. Stir in sherry and nutmeg. Pour cheese mixture into fondue pot and keep warm. Serve with bread, ham and apple cubes.

EGGS BENEDICT

for 1		for 2
1	English muffin(s), split and toasted	2
	butter	
2 slices	Canadian bacon or ham, sauteed	4 slices
1 tsp.	vinegar	2 tsp.
2	eggs	4
1/3 cup	Hollandaise Sauce, page 28	2/3 cup

Spread toasted English muffins with butter. Top each muffin half with one slice of Canadian bacon. Place in 200°F. oven and keep warm. Place water, to a depth of one inch, in a saucepan. add vinegar. Bring to a boil. Reduce heat to simmer. Gently break eggs into water. Cook 3 to 5 minutes, or to desired degree of doneness. Remove eggs with slotted spoon. Place one egg on each muffin half. Pour Hollandaise sauce over eggs. Serve immediately.

PASTA, RICE AND BREAD

Pasta, rice and bread can be called the "diplomats" of any meal. They blend together harmoniously with almost any dish, no matter how highly seasoned. And, they round out a dinner nicely by providing low cost nutrition that helps you stretch your food dollars.

Rice is great if you are making a meal that requires last-minute preparation. Cook it up to a week before you plan to serve it. About ten minutes before your meal, remove it from the refrigerator and place it in a small saucepan with a tablespoon or two of water. Cover and place over low heat. Stir occasionally with a fork until rice is hot.

PASTA

Perfect pasta can be yours, if you follow these directions. The oil added to the water prevents the pasta from sticking together and keeps the water from boiling over.

for 1		for 2
1 quart	water	2 quarts
1/4 tsp.	salt	1/2 tsp.
2 tsp.	oil	1 tbs.
2 ozs.	pasta	4 ozs.
	salt and pepper	

Bring water, salt and oil to boil in saucepan about twice the size as the amount of water called for. When a rolling boil has been achieved, add pasta. Boil uncovered until tender, but still offers a slight resistance to teeth when bitten. This is called "al dente." The time varies according to the type of pasta. Drain pasta in collander. Toss with one tablespoon of pesto or butter. Season with salt and freshly ground pepper.

PESTO

1 cup fresh basil leaves
2 cloves garlic
1 tbs. pine nuts (optional)
1/4 cup olive oil
2 tbs. grated Parmesan cheese

Place all ingredients in blender or food processor and blend until smooth. Use at once or freeze. Makes 1/3 cup.

BAKED NOODLES RICOTTA

A delicious side dish to serve with Veal Piccata on page 126.

A delicious side dish to serve with Veal Piccata on page 126.

for 1		for 2
1/2 cup	cooked noodles	1 cup
1-1/2 tsp.	melted butter	1 tbs.
1/4 cup	ricotta	1/2 cup
1/2	egg, beaten	1
dash	garlic powder (optional)	dash
	salt and pepper	
2 tbs.	grated Parmesan cheese	1/4 cup

Combine all ingredients in mixing bowl. Stir until blended. Place in 1 or 2 buttered ramekins. If desired, sprinkle with additional Parmesan cheese.* Bake in 350°F. oven for 20 minutes, or until hot and bubbly.

*May be made ahead to this point.

Hint: This dish freezes well for up to three weeks.

RICE

Replace the water in this recipe with beef or chicken broth for extra flavor.

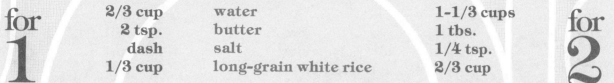

for 1			for 2
2/3 cup	water		1-1/3 cups
2 tsp.	butter		1 tbs.
dash	salt		1/4 tsp.
1/3 cup	long-grain white rice		2/3 cup

Combine water, butter and salt in saucepan. Bring to boil. Reduce heat to low. Add rice. Cover and cook for 20 minutes, or until liquid is absorbed and rice is tender.

Hint: Add any of the variations (or a combination) to the cooked rice:
• 1 tbs. slivered almonds
• 2 tbs. grated cheese
• 1 tsp. minced green onion or parsley
• 1/4 cup sauteed mushrooms

ARMENIAN RICE

Wonderful with lamb or chicken.

for 1			for 2
1 tsp.	butter		2 tsp.
1/4 coil	vermicelli, broken		1/2 coil
3 tbs.	long-grain rice		1/3 cup
	salt and pepper		
1/2 cup plus 2 tbs.	water		1-1/4 cups
1 tbs.	pine nuts (optional)		2 tbs.
	sauteed until golden in		
	2 tsp. butter		

Melt butter in skillet over medium heat. Add vermicelli and brown. Add rice, salt, pepper, water and bring to a boil. Reduce heat. Cover and cook over low heat for about 25 minutes, or until liquid is absorbed. Remove from heat and set aside for 5 minutes. Add pine nuts and serve.

BULGAR PILAFF

A nutritious alternative to rice — ideal with Shish Kabobs, on page 134.

on page 134

for 1		for 2
2 tsp.	butter	4 tsp.
1 tbs.	chopped onion	2 tbs.
1/4 cup	bulgar (cracked wheat)	1/2 cup
1/2 cup	chicken stock	1 cup
	dash cinnamon	
	dash celery seed	
1 tbs.	pine nuts (optional)	2 tbs.

Melt butter in saucepan over medium heat. Add onion and bulgar. Saute until golden. Add remaining ingredients and bring to boil. Reduce heat. Cover and cook over low heat for 15 minutes, or until liquid is absorbed. Stir in pine nuts.

RICE VERDE

This colorful rice dish is great served with Mexican food. Try it with our Tacos, on page 38.

for 1

		for 2
2/3 cup	cooked rice	1-1/3 cups
2 tbs.	sour cream	1/4 cup
1 tbs.	chopped green chilies or green onions	2 tbs.
1/4 cup	grated Cheddar or Monterey Jack cheese	1/2 cup

Place half the rice in buttered ramekin. Combine sour cream, chilies and half the cheese in mixing bowl. Spread over rice. Cover with remaining rice. Top with Cheese.* Bake in 350°F. oven for 15 minutes.

*May be made ahead to this point. Chill up to one day before baking.

BISCUITS

Piping hot biscuits melt in your mouth. For a delicious variation, press a sugar cube which has been dipped in orange juice into the center of each biscuit before it is baked.

1 cup flour
1-1/2 tsp. baking powder
1/4 tsp. salt
3 tbs. butter
1/3 cup milk

Stir flour, baking powder and salt together in a mixing bowl. Cut in butter until mixture resembles coarse cornmeal. Add milk and stir lightly. Knead gently twelve times. Roll or pat dough to 1/2-inch thickness. Cut into squares or rounds. Place on ungreased baking sheet. Bake in 450°F. oven for 12 minutes, or until golden brown. Makes 6 biscuits.

HOT CHEESE BREAD

Great with soup or salad!

1 tbs. butter, at room temperature
3 tbs. mayonnaise
2 tsp. sliced green onions or chopped chives
2 tsp. minced parsley
1/2 cup grated Cheddar cheese
2 French rolls or 4 slices French bread

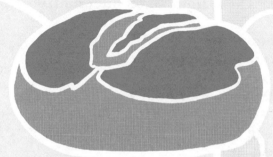

Combine butter, mayonnaise, onions, parsley and cheese in a mixing bowl. Stir until blended. Split rolls and spread with cheese mixture. Broil until bubbly. Makes 1/2 cup cheese spread.

MUFFINS

These light and tender muffins are best served hot from the oven.

1 cup flour
1 tsp. baking powder
1/4 tsp. salt
2 tbs. sugar or honey
1/4 cup milk
1 egg
3 tbs. oil

Stir dry ingredients together, making a well in the center. Combine liquid ingredients and add to dry ingredients. Stir until just moistened. Let sit for one minute. Fill greased or paper-lined muffin pans 2/3 full. Bake in 400°F. oven for 20 minutes, or until golden brown. Makes 6 muffins.

VARIATIONS

Stir one or more of the following ingredients into the batter before baking:

- 1 tbs. fried bacon, crumbled
- 1 tbs. thinly sliced green onion
- 1/4 cup shredded cheese, such as Swiss or Cheddar
- 1 tsp. grated orange or lemon peel
- 1/4 cup raisins and 1/2 tsp. cinnamon

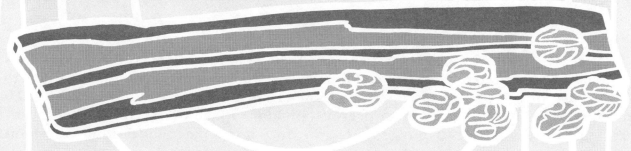

BASIC YEAST BREAD

This recipe yields one traditionally-sized loaf or three mini-loaves .

1/4 cup warm water
1 package yeast
1 cup milk
1 tbs. melted butter or oil
1 tsp. salt
1 tbs. honey, sugar or molasses
1-1/2 cups whole wheat flour }
1-1/2 cups all-purpose flour } or 3 cups all-purpose flour
1/4 cup wheat germ (optional)

Dissolve yeast in warm water. Scald milk and cool to lukewarm. Stir milk into yeast and add melted butter, salt and honey. Gradually blend in flour until dough is stiff. Place dough on floured board and knead until smooth and elastic, about 10 minutes. Add flour as needed to prevent sticking. Place dough in greased bowl, turning to coat top. Cover bowl and let rise in a warm place until doubled, about

1-1/2 hours. Punch dough down and form a loaf or loaves, pressing out air bubbles. Place in greased pan(s), cover, and let rise in a warm place until doubled, about 45 minutes. If desired, brush top of loaf with melted butter for a shiny crust. Bake in a 375°F. oven for 45 minutes, or until brown, for one 9 x 5 x 3-inch loaf. For three 6 x 3 x 2-inch loaves, bake 25 minutes. Place on racks to cool for 5 minutes. Remove from pans and let cool completely. Freezes well for up to two months.

VARIATIONS

HERB CHEESE BREAD — Add 1/4 cup grated Parmesan cheese, 1 tablespoon minced onion and 1 teaspoon of dill, basil or oregano to the flour mixture.
RYE BREAD — Omit 3 cups of all purpose flour and add instead 1 cup rye flour, 2 cups all purpose flour and 1 teaspoon of caraway seed.
CINNAMON RAISIN BREAD — Omit 1 tablespoon of honey and add instead 1/4 cup honey or sugar. Also, add 1/2 teaspoon cinnamon and 1/2 cup raisins to flour mixture.

VEGETABLES

When serving vegetables, carefully consider the meal they are to accompany. Their size, shape, color and flavor should complement, but not overpower the entree. For example, if the main course is Stuffed Trout, on page 164, sauteed mushrooms would not be a good vegetable choice. This is primarily because mushrooms are already included in the stuffing for the trout; also, mushrooms lack the color and texture to properly contrast with the fish. A much better vegetable choice would be Dilled Green Beans, on page 110, or Broccoli with Browned Butter, on page 109. To complete the meal, serve rice cooked in chicken broth, sprinkled with slivered almonds.

ARTICHOKES IN WHITE WINE

Select firm artichokes with tightly closed leaves. For variety, chill and stuff with Rice Salad, page 65. An excellent accompaniment to any lamb dish.

for 1		for 2
1	artichoke(s)	2
1/2 clove	garlic, chopped	1 clove
1 tsp.	chopped parsley	2 tsp.
	salt and pepper	
1 tbs.	olive oil	2 tbs.
1/4 cup	white wine	1/2 cup

Remove small outer leaves from bottom of artichoke(s). Cut off stems so artichoke(s) will set flat and cut off thorny tips of leaves with scissors. Place in small saucepan. Combine garlic, parsley, salt, pepper and oil. Spoon between leaves of artichoke(s). Pour wine into pan. Cover and simmer 45 to 60 minutes or until leaves pull off easily. Add water if necessary. To stuff cooked, chilled artichoke(s), spread leaves apart and scoop out choke using a teaspoon. Fill cavity with salad.

ASPARAGUS WITH MUSTARD SAUCE

Spoon mustard sauce over hot or chilled asparagus spears.

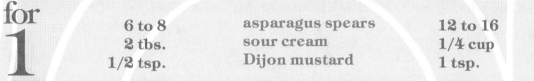

for 1

6 to 8	asparagus spears	12 to 16
2 tbs.	sour cream	1/4 cup
1/2 tsp.	Dijon mustard	1 tsp.

for 2

Snap tough ends off asparagus. Steam or boil in small amount of water for 10 minutes, or until just tender. Combine sour cream with mustard and spoon over asparagus.

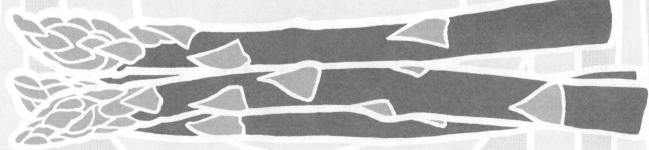

107

BAKED WINTER SQUASH

Any winter squash is delicious when spiced with nutmeg and glazed with molasses and brown sugar. Bake this along with Meat Loaf on page 120.

Bake this along with Meat Loaf on page 120.

for 1		for 2
1/2	acorn or other winter squash	1
1 tbs.	butter	2 tbs.
1 tsp.	molasses	2 tsp.
1 tsp.	brown sugar	2 tsp.
	dash nutmeg	
	salt and pepper	

Cut squash in half and scoop out seeds. Arrange, cut-side down, in shallow baking pan. Surround with a small amount of hot water. Bake in 350°F. oven 30 minutes. Combine butter, molasses, brown sugar and seasonings. Pour off liquid from baking pan. Turn squash cut-side up. Spread glaze over squash. Bake 30 minutes, or until tender, basting now and then with sauce.

BROCCOLI WITH BROWNED BUTTER

Broccoli becomes irresistable with a hint of nutmeg.

for
1

1 stalk	broccoli	2 stalks
1 tbs.	butter	2 tbs.
	dash nutmeg	
	salt and pepper	

for
2

Cut broccoli into flowerets. Steam or boil in small amount of water for 10 minutes, or until just tender. Melt butter with nutmeg over low heat until butter is light brown, not scorched. Pour butter over broccoli. Add salt and pepper as desired.

DILLED GREEN BEANS

Dill adds zest to tender green beans. This vegetable creation is great served with any seafood dish.

for 1		for 2
1 cup	fresh green beans, cut in 1-1/2-inch pieces	2 cups
2 tsp.	butter	1 tbs.
	dash dill	
1/2 tsp.	lemon juice	1 tsp.
	salt and pepper	

Boil green beans in small amount of water for 10 minutes, or until just tender. Drain well. Add butter, dill, lemon juice, salt and pepper. Stir until beans are well coated with seasonings.

GARLIC POTATO STRIPS

Roasted until golden, these garlic flavored potatoes go well with steaks, roast or chicken.

for 1

1	potato(es)	2
1 tbs.	butter	2 tbs.
1/2 clove	garlic, crushed	1 clove
	salt	

for 2

Quarter potato(es) lengthwise and peel, if desired. Boil for 10 minutes and drain. Melt butter in baking pan. Add garlic and potato strips turning to coat with butter and garlic. Sprinkle with salt. Bake in 350°F. oven for 45 minutes, turning once or twice.

GLAZED CARROTS

A hint of mustard accents these beautifully glazed carrots.

for 1		for 2
2 tsp.	butter	4 tsp.
3/4 cup	sliced carrots	1-1/2 cups
2 tsp.	brown sugar	4 tsp.
1/4 tsp.	prepared mustard	1/2 tsp.
	salt and pepper	

Melt butter in heavy saucepan or small skillet with a lid. Stir in remaining ingredients. Cover and simmer for 25 minutes, or until carrots are tender.

HERBED TOMATO

A delicious and colorful garnish for the meat platter.

1	tomato(es), halved	2
1 tsp.	butter	2 tsp.
	dash basil	
	dash oregano	
	salt and pepper	
	Parmesan cheese, grated	

Place tomato halves in baking pan. Dot each half with butter and sprinkle with herbs, salt, pepper and cheese.* Bake in 350°F. oven for 20 minutes, or broil for 3 minutes or until heated through and cheese is lightly browned. Watch carefully.

*May be made ahead to this point. Cover and refrigerate.

SCALLOPED POTATOES

Potatoes layered with cheese and ham make a meal when combined with a vegetable.

for 1		potato(es), peeled and sliced	for 2
1 medium		potato(es), peeled and sliced	2 medium
1 tbs.		flour	2 tbs.
		salt and pepper	
1 tsp.		minced onion	2 tsp.
1/4 cup		grated cheese	1/2 cup
1/4 cup		chopped, cooked ham (optional)	1/2 cup
1/2 cup		milk	1 cup
1 tsp.		butter	2 tsp.

Place half of potato slices in small buttered baking dish. Sprinkle with flour, salt, pepper, onion, cheese and ham. Top with remaining potato slices. Pour milk over all and dot with butter. Bake uncovered in 350°F. oven for 1 hour.

SUMMER SQUASH CASSEROLE

A delectable combination of flavors.

for 1		for 2
1 cup	summer squash, cubed	2 cups
1 tbs.	chopped onion	2 tbs.
1 tbs.	chopped green pepper	2 tbs.
1/4 cup	grated Cheddar cheese	1/2 cup
2 tbs.	sour cream	1/4 cup
3 tbs.	croutons	6 tbs.

Cook squash, onion and pepper in small amount of water until just tender. Drain vegetables well. Combine with cheese, sour cream and two-thirds of the croutons. Place in buttered ramekin. Top with remaining croutons.* Bake in 350° F. oven for 20 minutes or until hot and bubbly.

*May be made ahead to this point. Cover and refrigerate.

MEATS

With our imaginative recipes, tailored to serve one or two, you need not be limited to steaks and chops. Beef Carbonnade, Mock Ravioli and Veal Piccata are a few of our classic dishes. For convenience prepare our Ground Beef Mix for hamburgers, meat balls and meat loaf.

GROUND BEEF MIX
FOR HAMBURGERS, MEAT BALLS OR MEAT LOAF

For convenience prepare our make-ahead mix. Shape into patties, balls or loaves and freeze for future quick and easy meals.

MAKE-AHEAD MIX FOR 2

1/2 lb. ground beef
1 egg
2 tbs. bread crumbs or wheat germ
1 tbs. milk
2 tbs. chopped onion
1/4 tsp. salt
dash pepper

MAKE-AHEAD MIX FOR 8

2 lbs. ground beef
4 eggs
1/2 cup bread crumbs or wheat germ
1/4 cup milk
1/2 cup chopped onion
1 tsp. salt
1/4 tsp. pepper

VARIATIONS FOR 2

1/2 tsp. Worcestershire sauce
2 tbs. chopped parsley
1/4 cup grated cheese
1 tbs. chopped green pepper

VARIATIONS FOR 8

2 tsp. Worcestershire sauce
1/2 cup chopped parsley
1 cup grated cheese
1/4 cup chopped green pepper

Mix all ingredients together adding variations. Form into hamburger patties, meat balls or meat loaves. Make-Ahead Mix for 2 makes 2 hamburger patties or 12 meat balls, or 1 individual meat loaf. Make-Ahead Mix for 8 makes 8 hamburger patties, 48 meat balls or 1 large or 4 individual meat loaves. Freeze in serving-sized portions.

For hamburger patties fry 5 minutes on each side or broil 4 minutes on each side for medium doneness. Baste hamburgers with soy sauce or Barbeque Sauce, page 31, while cooking if desired. Serve in bun with traditional garnishes or top with any of the following: sauteed mushrooms, cheese, sour cream mixed with chopped chives or bacon bits, or Bearnaise Sauce, page 27.

For meat balls bake in 375°F. oven for 30 minutes or fry in 1 tablespoon oil for 10 minutes, turning to brown. Add cooked meat balls to Barbeque Sauce, page 31, or Sweet And Sour Sauce, page 30, and heat through.

For meatloaf place mix for 8 in large 9 x 5-inch baking pan. Bake in 350°F. oven about 1-1/2 hours. Place mix for 2 in one 6 x 3 x 2-inch loaf pan and bake in 350°F. oven for 45 minutes. If desired top with 1/4 cup Tomato Sauce, page 32, before baking.

SPAGHETTI SAUCE

Hot Cheese Bread, page 99, and a tossed green salad complete this favorite meal. If time allows make the sauce ahead—the flavor will be even better when reheated.

1/2 lb. ground beef
1/4 cup chopped onion
1/2 clove garlic, minced
1/2 cup sliced mushrooms
1 cup Tomato Sauce, page 32
dash oregano
dash basil
2 tbs. red wine

Brown meat and onions in frying pan over medium-high heat. Drain fat. Stir in remaining ingredients and simmer 30 minutes. Serve over hot cooked spaghetti. Makes 2 servings. For 1 serving refrigerate or freeze remaining half of sauce for another meal.

BEEF CARBONNADE

Beer adds flavor to this robust stew. Serve over hot, buttered noodles.

1 tbs. oil
1/2 lb. beef stew meat, cut in 1-inch cubes
1 small onion, sliced
1/2 clove garlic, chopped
1 tbs. flour
salt and pepper
1/2 cup beer
1 tbs. brown sugar
1/2 bay leaf
dash thyme

Heat oil in skillet. Brown meat. Remove from skillet and set aside. Add onions and garlic to skillet. Cook, stirring, until limp. Return meat to pan. Sprinkle with

122

flour and season with salt and pepper. Add remaining ingredients. Cover and simmer over low heat for 1-1/2 hours or until meat is tender, or bake in 325°F. oven for 1-1/2 hours. Makes 2 servings. For 1 serving, refrigerate or freeze remaining half for another meal.

STIR-FRIED BEEF AND VEGETABLES

A colorful blend of meat and vegetables to serve with rice.

for 1		for 2
1/4 lb.	beef steak, partially frozen for easy slicing	1/2 lb.
1 tbs.	soy sauce	2 tbs.
1 tsp.	sherry	2 tsp.
1 tsp.	oil	2 tsp.
1/4 tsp.	sugar	1/2 tsp.
	dash ginger	
1 tbs.	oil	2 tbs.
1/4 cup	carrot, sliced	1/2 cup
1	green onion(s)	2
1/2 cup	green beans	1 cup
1/2 cup	mushrooms	1 cup

Thinly slice steak. Combine soy sauce, sherry, oil, sugar and ginger. Pour over

meat. Set aside to marinate a few minutes. Slice vegetables thinly on the diagonal.
Heat 1 or 2 tablespoons oil in wok or frying pan. Add vegetables and stir-fry about
2 minutes until tender crisp. Remove from pan and set aside. Add meat to wok and
stir-fry quickly, about 30 seconds. Return vegetables to pan. Toss with meat and
serve immediately.

VEAL PICCATA

A delicious quick and easy favorite flavored with lemon and capers.

for 1		for 2
3 ozs.	sliced veal	6 ozs.
1 tbs.	flour	2 tbs.
	salt and pepper	
2 tsp.	butter	4 tsp.
2 tbs.	dry white wine	1/4 cup
1 tsp.	capers	2 tsp.
1 tsp.	lemon juice	2 tsp.

Pound veal slices to 1/4-inch thickness. Season flour with salt and pepper. Dredge meat in seasoned flour.* Saute veal in butter until lightly browned, one or two minutes per side. Remove to heated platter. Pour wine into frying pan. Bring to boil. Stir in capers and lemon juice. Pour sauce over veal and serve immediately.

*May be made ahead to this point. Cover and refrigerate for up to 1 day in advance.

MOCK RAVIOLI

1/2 lb. ground beef
1/4 cup chopped onion
1/2 clove garlic, minced
1 cup Tomato Sauce, page 32
dash oregano, basil, chili powder
  and sugar

1/2 cup sliced mushrooms
1 cup uncooked bow-tie macaroni
2 cups chopped fresh spinach
1 egg, beaten
1/4 cup Romano or
  Parmesan cheese, grated

Brown ground beef and onion in skillet over medium-high heat. Drain fat. Add garlic, Tomato Sauce, seasonings and mushrooms. Simmer 30 minutes. Cook macaroni in boiling salted water 10 minutes. Drain well. Combine cooked macaroni with spinach and egg. Spread half of meat sauce in baking dish. Add half of macaroni mixture. Spread remaining meat sauce over macaroni and top with remaining macaroni mixture. Sprinkle with cheese.* Bake in 350°F. oven for 30 minutes. Makes 2 servings. For 1 serving refrigerate or freeze half, either before or after baking, for another meal.

LAMB CHOPS RATATOUILLE

for 1		for 2
1	lamb chop(s), well trimmed	2
1/2 cup	sliced zucchini	1 cup
1/2 cup	chopped eggplant	1 cup
1/2 clove	garlic, chopped	1 clove
1 tbs.	chopped onion	2 tbs.
1/4 cup	chopped tomato	1/2 cup
	dash thyme	
	dash basil	
	salt and pepper	

Place lamb chop on square of aluminum foil. Top with remaining ingredients. Bring ends of foil together and loosely fold to form package with opening at top to allow steam to escape.* Bake in 350°F. oven for 1 hour, or until meat is tender. If desired, meat and vegetables may be baked in covered baking dish.

*May be made ahead to this point. Cover and refrigerate for up to a day in advance.

129

SWISS STEAK

Meat braised in a savory vegetable sauce is marvelous with mashed potatoes.

1/2 lb. round steak
2 tbs. flour
salt and pepper
1 tbs. oil
1 small onion, sliced
1 cup sliced carrots
1/4 cup chopped green pepper
1 cup Tomato Sauce, page 32
salt and pepper

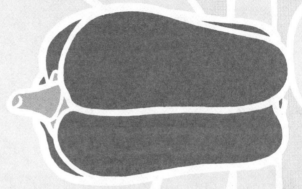

Mix flour with salt and pepper. Pound into meat. Heat oil in skillet over medium-high heat. Brown meat. Remove to baking dish. Top with vegetables, Tomato Sauce, salt and pepper. Cover and bake in 350°F. oven for 1 hour or until meat is tender. Makes 2 servings. For 1 serving, refrigerate or freeze remaining half for another meal.

STEAK AU POIVRE

Complete your menu with Garlic Potato Strips, page 111, Asparagus with Mustard Sauce, page 107, and Chocolate Mousse, page 169.

for 1			for 2
6 ozs.	beef sirloin		12 ozs.
2 tbs.	coarsely ground black pepper		1/4 cup
	salt		
1 tbs.	cognac		2 tbs.
1 tbs.	cream		2 tbs.

Cut steak into serving pieces. Press pepper into meat. Sprinkle salt over bottom of heavy skillet and place over high heat. When salt begins to brown, add steak and cook over high heat for several minutes. Turn steak, lower heat, and cook to desired doneness. Pour cognac over steak and ignite. When flames die, remove steak to heated plate. Add cream to skillet and cook stirring until thickened. Pour sauce over steak.

ORANGE PORK CHOPS

Sweet potato and orange slices complement the flavor of pork in this recipe.

for 1			for 2
1	pork chop(s)	2	
1-1/2 tsp.	oil	1 tbs.	
1/2	sweet potato or yam, peeled	1	
1/4	orange, sliced	1/2	
	dash cinnamon		
	salt and pepper		

Brown pork in hot oil. Cut sweet potato in 1/2 inch slices. Place meat and sweet potato slices in baking dish. Cover with orange slices.* Bake covered in 350°F. oven for 1 hour, or until meat is tender.

*May be made ahead to this point. Cover and refrigerate for up to 1 day in advance.

PORK CHOPS WITH BROWN RICE

for 1

for 1		for 2
1-1/2 tsp.	oil	1 tbs.
1	pork chop(s)	2
1/2 cup	beef broth	1 cup
2 tbs.	dry white wine	1/4 cup
1/2	carrot, cut into julienne strips	1
2 tbs.	chopped onion	1/4 cup
	dash marjoram	
	dash oregano	
	salt and pepper	
1/4 cup	brown rice	1/2 cup

for 2

Heat oil in skillet over medium-high heat. Brown meat well. Remove from pan and set aside. Drain excess fat from pan. Add broth, wine, carrot, onion and seasonings to pan and bring to boil. Stir in rice. Arrange chops over all. * Cover and bake in 350°F. oven for 1 hour or until liquid is absorbed.

*May be made ahead to this point. Cover and refrigerate for up to 1 day in advance.

133

SHISH KABOBS

for 1			for 2
1/3 lb.		lamb or beef, cut in 1-inch cubes	2/3 lb.

LAMB MARINADE

1 tbs.		lemon juice	2 tbs.
2 tbs.		olive oil	1/4 cup
1/2 clove		garlic, chopped	1 clove
		dash thyme	

BEEF MARINADE

1 tbs.		red wine	2 tbs.
2 tbs.		olive oil	1/4 cup
1/2 clove		garlic, chopped	1 clove
1/2		bay leaf, crumbled	1

VEGETABLES

mushrooms
cherry tomatoes
green pepper slices
pineapple chunks
zucchini slices
eggplant cubes
onion wedges

Trim fat from meat. Combine ingredients for desired marinade. Add meat and marinate several hours or overnight. Drain, reserving marinade. Select 2 or 3 vegetables and thread on skewers with meat. Broil 4 inches from heat for 8 minutes, or barbeque over hot coals for 10 minutes. Turn and baste with reserved marinade.

SPARERIBS

Be prepared to eat these with your fingers!

for 1

1 lb.   country-style spareribs   2 lbs.
1/2 recipe   Barbeque Sauce, page 31   1 recipe

for 2

Place ribs in roasting pan meat side up. Roast in 450°F. oven for 25 minutes. Drain off all fat. Pour sauce over ribs. Bake in 350°F. oven for 1 hour or barbeque over medium coals for 30 to 40 minutes. Baste ribs occasionally and add water if sauce becomes too thick.

136

LAMB STEW

1/2 lb. lamb for stew, cubed (1 lb. lamb shoulder chops)
1 cup chicken stock
1/4 cup chopped onion
1 bay leaf
salt and pepper
dill, dash
1 potato, cubed
2 carrots, sliced
1 small rutabaga, peeled and cubed, or 1 cup shredded cabbage
2 tbs. water
1 tbs. flour

Combine lamb, stock and seasonings in a saucepan. Bring to a boil, reduce heat and simmer 1 hour. Add vegetables and simmer 30 minutes or until meat and vegetables are tender. Blend flour and water together to form a paste. Add to stew, stirring until thickened. Makes 2 servings. For 1 serving, refrigerate or freeze remaining half for another meal.

137

POULTRY

We usually recommend buying foods in single- or double-portion servings. However, when it comes to chicken, buy a whole one. You can save money by cutting it up yourself. And, one chicken makes at least two meals for two people. The breast, thighs and legs can be made into a number of dishes, fried chicken, broiled chicken, barbecued chicken, etc. Leftovers from these dishes can be made into crepes, omelets, soups or sandwiches. Less savory parts, such as the wings, bones or skin can be made into chicken stock. Simply cover them with water and add a stalk of celery, a bay leaf and a few peppercorns to the water. Simmer for about two hours. Strain liquid and discard seasonings. Place in the refrigerator overnight and discard hardened fat the next day. Use stock in other recipes or make it into soup by adding diced chicken, vegetables, rice or noodles. For the cost of one chicken and a little work, just think of all the money you have saved!

OVEN FRIED CHICKEN

Traditionally served with hot biscuits and honey. A good take-along for a picnic.

for 1		for 2
3/4 lb.	chicken pieces	1-1/2 lbs.
2 tbs.	bread crumbs or wheat germ	1/4 cup
2 tbs.	Parmesan cheese	1/4 cup
1/8 tsp.	paprika	1/4 tsp.
1/8 tsp.	salt	1/4 tsp.
	pepper	
2 tbs.	buttermilk or melted butter	1/4 cup

Wash chicken and dry with paper towels. Combine bread crumbs with cheese and seasonings. Dip chicken in buttermilk then roll in crumb mixture. Place in well-buttered baking dish.* Bake in 350°F. oven for 1 hour.

*May be made ahead to this point. Cover and refrigerate for up to a day in advance.

COQ AU VIN

for 1		for 2
1 tsp.	oil	2 tsp.
2 tbs.	chopped onion	1/4 cup
1/2 small clove	garlic, minced	1 small clove
3/4 lbs.	chicken pieces	1-1/2 lbs.
1-1/2 tsp.	flour	1 tbs.
1-1/2 tsp.	minced parsley	1 tbs.
1/4	bay leaf	1/2
pinch	thyme	1/8 tsp.
	salt and pepper	
1/2	sliced carrot	1
1/2 cup	sliced fresh mushrooms	1 cup
1 cup	red wine	2 cups

Place oil in skillet over medium-high heat. Saute onion and garlic. Add chicken and brown well on all sides. Sprinkle with flour and seasonings. Add carrot, mushrooms and wine. Cover and simmer 1 hour.

141

BAKED OR BROILED CHICKEN

Baste the chicken with either the Lemon-Herb Sauce or the Teriyaki Sauce. Use leftover chicken for the Chicken Sauce, page 150, or Chicken and Fruit Salad, page 62.

for 1

3/4 lb.   chicken pieces   1-1/2 lbs.   **for 2**
                 salt and pepper
                 Sauce (see next page)

Place chicken skin-side down on baking or broiler pan. Sprinkle with salt and pepper and brush with desired sauce. Bake in 375°F. oven for 20 minutes. Turn chicken and brush again with sauce. Bake 20 to 25 minutes longer, or until done. Or broil for 15 minutes, until lightly browned. Turn chicken, brush with sauce and broil 15 minutes longer, or until done.

LEMON-HERB SAUCE

for 1
for 2

1 tbs.	melted butter	2 tbs.
1 tbs.	lemon juice	2 tbs.
1/4 tsp.	tarragon or rosemary	1/2 tsp.

Mix together well.

TERIYAKI SAUCE

1 tbs.	soy sauce	2 tbs.
1 tbs.	sherry	2 tbs.
1 tbs.	honey	2 tbs.

Mix together well.

143

CHICKEN MORAGA

To complete this meal we suggest a tossed salad, your favorite pasta and Lemon Pudding, page 177, for dessert.

for 1			for 2
3/4 lb.	chicken pieces	1-1/2 lbs.	
2 tbs.	flour	1/4 cup	
1/8 tsp.	salt	1/4 tsp.	
	pepper		
1-1/2 tsp.	oil	1 tbs.	
2 tbs.	chopped onion	1/4 cup	
2 tbs.	sliced green pepper	1/4 cup	
1/2 cup	sliced fresh mushrooms	1 cup	
1/2 clove	garlic, minced	1 clove	
1/2 cup	Tomato Sauce, page 32	1 cup	
	dash oregano		

Place chicken in plastic bag with flour, salt and pepper. Shake to coat. Place oil in skillet over medium-high heat. Brown chicken and set aside. Saute onions, green

144

pepper, mushrooms and garlic in pan drippings. Add chicken, tomato sauce and oregano. Cover and simmer 1 hour, or place in baking dish* and bake in 350°F. oven for 1 hour.

*May be made ahead to this point. Cover and refrigerate for up to 1 day in advance.

STUFFED CHICKEN BREASTS

Cheese and herbs melt inside the tender chicken breast.

for
1
for
2

for 1		for 2
1 whole	chicken breast(s), skinned and boned	2 whole
	salt and pepper	
2 tbs.	soft butter	1/4 cup
	dash oregano	
1/2 tsp.	chopped parsley	1 tsp.
1 slice	Monterey Jack or Swiss cheese	2 slices
2 tbs.	flour	1/4 cup
1	egg, beaten	1
2 tbs.	bread crumbs or wheat germ	1/4 cup
2 tbs.	dry white wine	1/4 cup

Pound chicken between 2 pieces of wax paper until thin. Season with salt and pepper. Combine butter with herbs. Spread mixture on chicken. Place slice of cheese on each piece of chicken and roll. Secure with toothpick, if desired. Dip chicken in flour, egg and bread crumbs.* Bake in 375°F. oven for 15 minutes. Pour wine over chicken and bake 25 minutes longer.

*May be made ahead to this point. Cover and refrigerate up to a day in advance.

CORNISH GAME HENS
WITH ORANGE NUT STUFFING

The perfect choice for a company dinner.

for 1

1	Rock Cornish game hen(s)	2	
1 tbs.	melted butter	2 tbs.	
2 tbs.	red currant jelly, melted	1/4 cup	

for 2

Rinse hen(s) and pat dry with paper towels. Stuff hen(s) with Orange Nut Stuffing. Place breast-side up on rack in roasting pan. Brush with melted butter. Bake in 350°F. oven for 1 hour or until legs move easily. Brush hen(s) with jelly several times during last 15 minutes of baking time to glaze.

148

ORANGE NUT STUFFING

for 1

		for 2
1-1/2 tsp.	melted butter	1 tbs.
1-1/2 tsp.	chopped onion	1 tbs.
1/4 cup	long grain, brown or wild rice	1/2 cup
1/2 cup	water	1 cup
1 tsp.	grated orange	2 tsp.
1-1/2 tsp.	chopped parsley	1 tbs.
2 tbs.	chopped nuts	1/4 cup
dash	poultry seasoning	1/4 tsp.
	dash salt	

Saute onion in butter until tender. Add water and bring to boil. Stir in remaining ingredients. Reduce heat to low. Cover and cook until water is absorbed. Stuff hens.

149

CHICKEN SAUCE

for 1		for 2
1 tbs.	butter	2 tbs.
2 tbs.	chopped onion	1/4 cup
2 tbs.	sliced celery	1/4 cup
1 tbs.	flour	2 tbs.
1/4 cup	chicken broth	1/2 cup
1/4 cup	white wine	1/2 cup
	salt and pepper	
1/8 tsp.	tarragon or sage	1/4 tsp.
1 tbs.	chopped parsley	2 tbs.
1/2 cup	cooked chicken or turkey, cubed	1 cup

Saute onion in butter until tender. Stir in flour. Add chicken broth and wine gradually, cooking and stirring until thickened. Add remaining ingredients.* Heat through.

*May be made ahead to this point. Cover and refrigerate for up to four days.

ROAST TURKEY BREAST WITH CRANBERRY GLAZE

A holiday dinner for one or two with just enough leftovers for a couple of sandwiches.

1 turkey breast
salt
1 tbs. melted butter or oil
1/2 cup cranberry sauce
1 tbs. brown sugar
1 tsp. lemon juice

Place turkey on rack in roasting pan with skin-side up. Sprinkle with salt and brush with melted butter. Roast in 325°F. oven 25 minutes to the pound, or until meat thermometer registers 170°F. In a small bowl combine cranberry sauce, brown sugar and lemon juice. During last 15 minutes of roasting time brush turkey several times with mixture of cranberry sauce, brown sugar and lemon juice.

TURKEY CASSEROLE

for 1		for 2
1-1/2 tsp.	butter	1 tbs.
1-1/2 tsp.	flour	1 tbs.
1/4 cup	chicken broth	1/2 cup
1/4 cup	milk	1/2 cup
	dash pepper	
1/4 cup	brown or wild rice	1/2 cup
1/2 cup	diced turkey	1 cup
	or chicken	
1/4 cup	sliced fresh mushrooms	1/2 cup
1 tbs.	chopped green pepper	2 tbs.
2 tbs.	sliced almonds	1/4 cup

Melt butter in saucepan over medium-high heat. Add flour and blend. Stir in broth and milk. Cook, stirring, until thickened. Add remaining ingredients except almonds. Pour into buttered baking dish and sprinkle with almonds. Cover and bake in 350°F. oven for 1 hour or until rice is tender.

CHICKEN LIVERS IN PORT WINE

The flavors in this recipe blend to create a rich sauce. Serve with rice.

for 1		for 2
1 tbs.	minced onion	2 tbs.
1 tbs.	butter	2 tbs.
1/4 lb.	chicken livers	1/2 lb.
1 tbs.	flour	2 tbs.
1/4 cup	chicken broth	1/2 cup
3 tbs.	Port wine	6 tbs.
	salt and pepper	
1/2 cup	fresh or frozen peas	1 cup

Saute onion in butter over medium-high heat until tender. Add livers and cook 5 minutes, or until brown on all sides. Stir in flour. Add broth, Port, salt and pepper. Simmer 5 minutes. Add peas and cook 5 minutes longer. Serve over rice.

TURKEY TETRAZINNI

2 tbs. butter
1-1/2 cups sliced fresh mushrooms
1/4 cup finely chopped green pepper
1-1/2 tbs. flour
1 tsp. salt
dash pepper
1-1/4 cups half and half
2 cups diced cooked turkey or chicken
2 tbs. sherry
dash Tabasco sauce
3 ozs. uncooked spaghetti
1 egg yolk
1 tbs. (or more) grated Parmesan cheese

Melt butter in skillet over medium heat. Saute mushrooms and pepper 5 minutes. Blend in flour, salt and pepper. Add cream, stirring constantly. Cook until thickened. Add turkey and sherry. Heat through. Season with Tabasco sauce. Cook

154

spaghetti according to directions on page 90. Drain. Pour into shallow, greased baking dish. Add small amount of turkey mixture to egg yolk. Stir vigorously. Add remaining turkey mixture. Stir until blended. Pour over spaghetti. Sprinkle with cheese. Bake at 300°F. for 30 minutes. Makes 2 servings. For 1 serving, refrigerate or freeze half and serve for another meal.

SEAFOOD

High in protein and low in fat, seafood is becoming increasingly popular throughout the country. Although it is at its peak when fresh, properly frozen seafood is a close second. If you are buying fresh fish, always choose ones that have no objectionable odor. Contrary to popular belief, fresh fish don't "smell." Also, the flesh should spring back when touched with a finger and the scales should be adhered tightly to to the skin. If a fish can't pass these tests, don't buy it; it isn't fresh.

If you get to the market and can't find the type of fish your recipe calls for, don't worry. Fortunately, almost any fish can be substituted with another of similar fat content, flavor and texture. Your fishmonger can help you determine this.

One more hint: don't overcook fish. Unlike many meats, fish is naturally tender. It need only be cooked until the flesh firms slightly and can be flaked with a fork. Serve it immediately after it is cooked.

BAKED FISH

This easy recipe gives you a choice of two sauces.

for 1			for 2
6 ozs.	fish fillets		3/4 lb.
	butter		
	salt and pepper		
	Sauce (see next page)		
	lemon wedges		

Place fish in buttered baking dish. Sprinkle with salt and pepper and top with the sauce of your choice. Bake in 350°F. oven for 25 minutes, or until fish flakes easily when tested with a fork. Garnish with lemon wedges.

158

LEMON-PARSLEY SAUCE

for 1

		for 2
1 tbs.	melted butter	2 tbs.
2 tsp.	minced parsley	4 tsp.
2 tsp.	lemon juice	4 tsp.

Mix ingredients together well.

DILL-SOUR CREAM SAUCE

2 tbs.	sour cream	1/4 cup
1/2 tsp.	chopped chives	1 tsp.
	dash dill	

Mix ingredients together well.

159

SCALLOPS

for 1		for 2
1/4 lb.	scallops	1/2 lb.
1 tbs.	milk	2 tbs.
2 tbs.	bread crumbs or wheat germ	1/4 cup
	salt and pepper	
2 tsp.	butter	4 tsp.
1/2 clove	garlic, minced	1 clove
2 tbs.	white wine	1/4 cup
1 tsp.	chopped parsley	2 tsp.
	lemon wedges	

Rinse scallops and pat dry with paper towels. Dip in milk and coat with bread crumbs which have been seasoned with salt and pepper. Melt butter in skillet over medium-high heat. Add garlic and breaded scallops and saute until golden brown. Add wine and simmer one minute. Sprinkle with parsley and garnish with lemon wedges.

RED SNAPPER ALMONDINE

You may substitute fillet of sole for the red snapper in this recipe.

for
1

6 ozs.	red snapper fillets	3/4 lb.
1 tbs.	milk	2 tbs.
2 tbs.	bread crumbs or wheat germ	1/4 cup
	salt and pepper	
1 tbs.	butter	2 tbs.
1 tbs.	slivered almonds	2 tbs.

for
2

Dip fillets in milk then coat with bread crumbs which have been seasoned with salt and pepper. Melt butter in skillet over medium-high heat. Saute fillets in butter until golden brown and fish flakes easily when tested with a fork. Remove fish to heated serving plate. Saute almonds in pan drippings and spoon over fish.

SHRIMP RAMEKINS

for 1		for 2
1 tbs.	butter	2 tbs.
1 tbs.	flour	2 tbs.
1/3 cup	hot milk	2/3 cup
1 tsp.	chopped chives	2 tsp.
1 cup	cooked and deveined shrimp	2 cups
1 tbs.	sherry	2 tbs.
	salt and pepper	
1 tsp.	bread crumbs or wheat germ	2 tsp.
1 tsp.	grated Parmesan cheese	2 tsp.

Melt butter in small saucepan over medium heat. Stir in flour until blended. Quickly stir in milk and cook, stirring, until thickened. Add chives, shrimp, sherry, salt and pepper. Spoon into buttered ramekins or baking shells. Sprinkle with bread crumbs and cheese. Bake in 350°F. oven for 15 minutes.

SAVORY SALMON

Serve with Hollandaise Sauce, page 28, for an elegant meal.

<table>
<tr><td rowspan="5">for
1</td><td>1</td><td>salmon steak(s)</td><td>2</td><td rowspan="5">for
2</td></tr>
<tr><td>1 tsp.</td><td>butter</td><td>2 tsp.</td></tr>
<tr><td></td><td>salt and pepper</td><td></td></tr>
<tr><td></td><td>dash dill and tarragon</td><td></td></tr>
<tr><td>1 tsp.</td><td>capers</td><td>2 tsp.</td></tr>
</table>

Place salmon in buttered baking dish. Dot with butter and sprinkle with seasonings. Cover and bake in 400°F. oven for 15 minutes, or until salmon flakes when tested with a fork.

163

STUFFED TROUT

Mushrooms and lemon enhance the delicate flavor of trout in this recipe.

for 1			for 2
1 medium		trout	2 medium
		salt and pepper	
1 tbs.		butter	2 tbs.
1/4 cup		chopped mushrooms	1/2 cup
1/2 tsp.		lemon juice	1 tsp.
1 tsp.		chopped parsley	2 tsp.

Sprinkle cavity of trout with salt and pepper and dot with butter. Combine mushrooms, lemon juice and parsley. Spoon into cavity. Place trout in buttered baking dish. Bake in 375°F. oven for 20 minutes or until fish flakes easily when tested with a fork.

TUNA SAUCE

Spoon over freshly baked popovers or toast and sprinkle with paprika.

<table>
<tr><td>for 1</td><td></td><td></td><td>for 2</td></tr>
</table>

for 1			for 2
1/4 cup	sour cream		1/2 cup
1/4 tsp.	Worcestershire sauce		1/2 tsp.
1/2 tsp.	minced onion		1 tsp.
	dash pepper		
1/2 can	1 can (7 ozs.) tuna, drained		1 can
	dash paprika		
	parsley		

Combine sour cream, Worcestershire sauce and onion in small saucepan. Place over medium-high heat. Stir until mixture is hot, but do not allow to boil. Separate tuna into pieces. Add to sour cream mixture. Stir gently to avoid breaking tuna up too much. Heat to serving temperature. Spoon over toast. Dust with paprika and garnish with parsley. Serve immediately.

DESSERTS

You could make an entire cake or pie, but how many pieces of it are you really going to enjoy? Suppose you only want two pieces. What happens to the rest? You either throw it out after it becomes stale, and feel guilty, or eat all of it and feel virtuous, if overstuffed. We'll show you some favorite dessert recipes created especially for one or two. You'll be able to make the amount of dessert that is right for you.

Don't forget, fresh fruit and cheese make an excellent dessert. Grapes, apples and pears are the traditional accompaniments for cheese. Brie, Camembert, Teleme, Cheddar and blue cheese are all good to serve after dinner. It is also nice to add a few slices of French bread or crackers to your cheese board.

167

FRESH FRUIT FOR DESSERT

- Fresh fruits make an easy and nutritious finale to any meal. A basket of colorful fruits can serve as a centerpiece as well as dessert.
- Serve an assortment of fruits and cheeses with crackers, nuts and dates.
- Serve sliced fresh fruits topped with sour cream and brown sugar, sherbet, soft ice cream, whipped cream, yogurt and honey, granola, coconut, raisins, or dates, just to mention a few.
- Marinate sliced fresh fruit in wine or liqueur for a few minutes.
- Top ice cream or sherbet with sliced fresh fruit.
- Squeeze lemon or lime juice over melon or papaya.
- Garnish fresh fruit with a sprig of mint and sprinkle with slices almonds or walnuts.
- Combine 1/4 cup sour cream with 1 tablespoon brown sugar or honey, and 1 teaspoon lemon juice. Use as a dip for strawberries or grapes.

CHOCOLATE MOUSSE

This Mousse is ultra chocolaty. If you prefer a lighter Mousse, add only half the amount of chocolate and/or fold in 1/2 cup or more of whipped cream. Serve in your most glamorous stemware.

for 1

			for 2
1 oz.	semi-sweet chocolate	2 ozs.	
1 tbs.	water	2 tbs.	
1	egg yolk(s)	2	
2 tbs.	sugar	1/4 cup	
1	egg white(s), stiffly beaten	2	

Place chocolate and water in top of double boiler. Heat over barely simmering water until chocolate melts. Stir until blended. Set aside to cool. Beat egg yolk(s) and sugar until pale yellow and creamy. Beat in chocolate until well blended. Fold egg white(s) into chocolate mixture. Pour mousse into individual goblets or dessert dishes. Chill several hours or overnight.

FRESH FRUIT SHERBET

Cool and refreshing on a warm summer's evening.

1 cup fully ripened strawberries, blackberries, raspberries or peaches
1/4 cup sugar or more if fruit is tart
1/2 cup buttermilk
1 egg white, stiffly beaten

    Puree fruit in blender or food processor. Mix in sugar and let stand 10 minutes. Stir in buttermilk and fold in beaten egg white. Pour into ice cube trays or other freezer container and place in freezer. Stir sherbet gently every 2 hours, until firm.

170

BAKED APPLES

Delicious warm or cold. Great for breakfast as well as for dessert. For a super treat serve with sweetened cream, either plain or whipped.

for 1			for 2
1	baking apple(s), cored	2	
1 tbs.	brown sugar	2 tbs.	
2 tsp.	chopped walnuts	1 tbs.	
1 tbs.	chopped dates or raisins	2 tbs.	
	cinnamon		
1 tsp.	butter	2 tsp.	

Wash and core apple(s). Combine brown sugar, walnuts and dates. Fill apple(s) with mixture. Sprinkle with cinnamon and dot with butter. Place in baking dish.* Add water to just cover bottom of dish. Bake in 350°F. oven for 45 minutes or until apple(s) are tender.

*May be made ahead to this point. Cover and refrigerate.

BROWNIES

Our favorite brownies. They freeze well, too.

1/4 cup butter
1/2 cup sugar
2 eggs
1 can (5.5 ozs.) Hershey's chocolate syrup
1/2 cup flour
1/2 tsp. vanilla
dash salt
1/2 cup chopped nuts

Cream butter and sugar. Beat eggs in well. Add remaining ingredients and stir until blended. Pour batter into greased and floured 8 x 8 x 2-inch baking pan. Bake in 350°F. oven for 40 minutes. Cool and frost. When frosting is set cut into squares.

FROSTING

1/2 cup sugar
3 tbs. milk
1/4 cup semi-sweet chocolate chips

Combine sugar and milk in small saucepan. Boil for 5 minutes, or until mixture reaches soft ball stage, stirring occasionally. Add chocolate chips and stir until melted. Spread frosting over cooled brownies.

FRESH FRUIT TARTS

SINGLE CRUST TARTS (Makes 2)

1/2 cup flour
dash salt
3 tbs. butter or margarine
1 tbs. ice water

DOUBLE CRUST TARTS (Makes 2)

3/4 cup flour
1/4 tsp. salt
4 tbs. butter or margarine
2 tbs. ice water

Combine flour and salt. Cut in butter until mixture resembles coarse cornmeal. Stir in water with fork until dough holds together. Form two balls for single crust tarts or four balls for double crust tarts. Flatten balls, wrap in plastic and chill for 25 minutes.

For single crust tarts, roll pastry out on floured surface into two 6-1/2-inch rounds to fit 4-1/2-inch tart pans. Fit pastry into pans and flute edges. Fill with fruit, sprinkle with Crumb Topping, page 176, and bake in 400°F. oven for 30 to 40 minutes. For baked shells prick pastry with fork, and bake unfilled in a 450°F. oven for 10 to 12 minutes, or until golden. Fill as desired.

For double crust tarts, roll pastry out on floured surface into two 6-1/2-inch rounds. Fit into 4-1/2-inch tart pans. Roll remaining pastry into two rounds large enough to cover tops of tarts. Lay over filling. Flute edges, prick with fork and sprinkle with sugar. Bake in 400°F. oven for 30 to 40 minutes until crust is golden.

APPLE	APRICOT	BLACKBERRY	PEACH
2 cups apples peeled, cored, and sliced	1 cup apricots pitted	2 cups blackberries	2 cups peaches peeled, pitted, and sliced
1/4 cup sugar	1/3 cup sugar	1/4 cup sugar	1/3 cup sugar
1 tbs. flour or tapioca	1 tbs. flour or tapioca	1 tbs. flour or tapioca	1 tbs. flour or tapioca
1/4 tsp. cinnamon			1/4 tsp. cinnamon

Combine fruit with sugar, flour and spice. Spoon fruit mixture into prepared pastry shells. Sprinkle with Crumb Topping or, if making double crust tarts, top

175

with pastry. Finish and bake as directed.

CRUMB TOPPING

1/4 cup flour
2 tbs. brown sugar
2 tbs. butter
2 tbs. rolled oats or chopped nuts (optional)

Combine flour and sugar, and cut in butter. Add rolled oats, if desired. Sprinkle topping over single crust tarts. Bake in 400°F. oven for 30 to 40 minutes.

FRUIT CRISP

Arrange fruit mixture in individual baking dishes without crust. Top with Crumb Topping. Bake in 400°F. oven for 30 minutes.

LEMON PUDDING

A light dessert.

1 egg yolk
1/3 cup sugar
1-1/2 tsp. melted butter
1 tbs. flour
juice and grated peel of 1/2 lemon
1/2 cup milk
1 egg white, stiffly beaten

Mix egg yolk, sugar, butter, flour, lemon juice, peel and milk. Fold in egg white. Pour into two 6-ounce custard cups. Set in pan of water to depth of 1 inch. Bake in 350°F. oven for 40 minutes. Serve warm or cold. Unmold onto plate if desired. Makes 2 servings.

INDEX

183